Generations on the Land

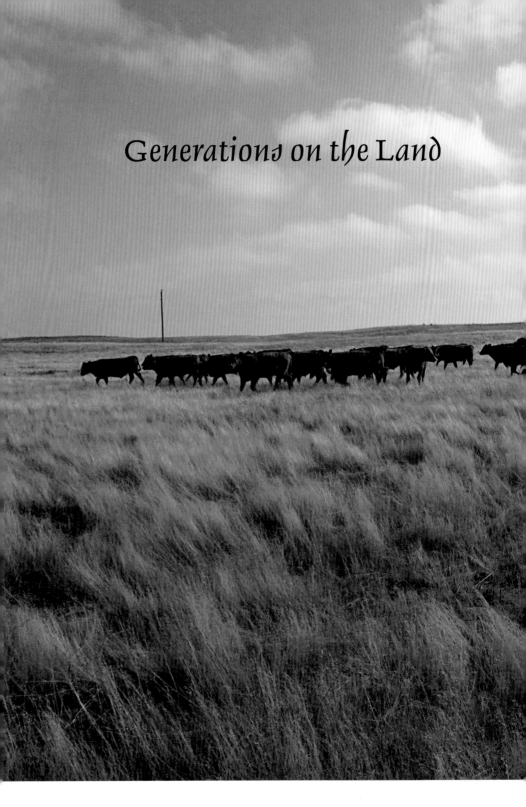

Generations on the Land

JOE NICK PATOSKI

With support from Sand County Foundation

A CONSERVATION LEGACY

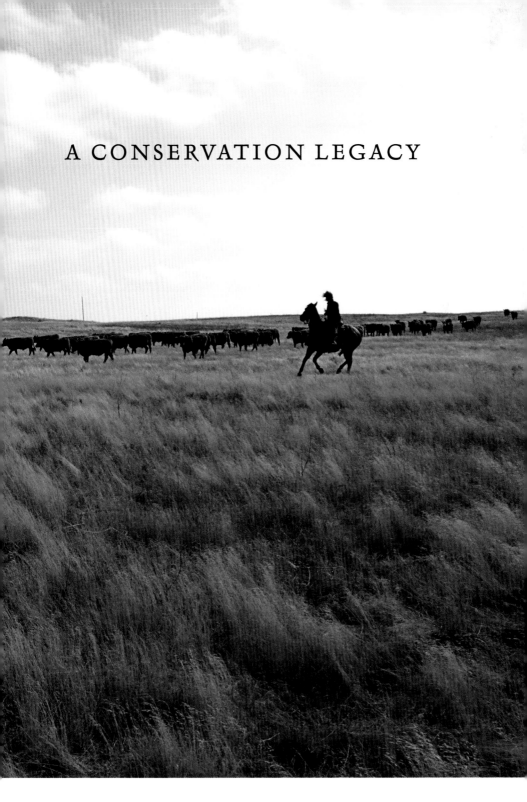

TEXAS A&M UNIVERSITY PRESS   COLLEGE STATION

© 2010 by Sand County Foundation

Manufactured in the China by Everbest Printing Inc.,

through FCI Print Group

First edition

This paper meets the requirements of

ANSI/NISO Z39.48-1992

(Permanence of Paper).

Binding materials have been chosen for durability.

LIBRARY OF CONGRESS CATALOGING-IN-PUBLICATION DATA

Patoski, Joe Nick, 1951–

Generations on the land : a conservation legacy / Sand County Foundation.—1st ed.

p. cm.

Includes index.

ISBN 978-1-60344-241-1 (cloth : alk. paper)

ISBN-10: 1-60344-241-3 (cloth : alk. paper)

1. Land use—Environmental aspects—United States.   2. Landowners—United
States—Biography.   3. Sustainable agriculture—United States.   4. Conservation
of natural resources—United States.   5. Natural resources—United States—
Management.   6. Leopold Conservation Award.

I. Sand County Foundation.   II. Title.

HD108.3.P38   2011

333.730973—dc22

2010026438

Contents

Foreword

When I am a noteworthy landowner family's guest, I find many delights in the visit and conversations. If my time and their hospitality permit, I like to take a walk before breakfast—preferably a hike—past their barn, machine shop, and sheds out to and beyond a close-in pasture. If time is short, a stroll from the farm or ranch headquarters out to the main road can suffice. I prefer, though, to turn toward the hills or the creek bank, not the main gate. As Aldo Leopold noted, "the back 40" is often the area where the landowners' signatures are written most sharply on their land. Thus, I walk, and I look for how tools may have been used by that family or its predecessors.

Why do I look for the effects of landowners' tools? Because tools are the means by which people convert intention into action, impulse into creation or damage. Consideration of how tools are deployed was one of the critical concerns of Aldo Leopold, a conservation philosopher in whose honor the Leopold Conservation Award program was created by Sand County Foundation.

> The central thesis of game management is this: game can be restored by the creative use of the same tools which have heretofore destroyed it—axe, plow, cow, fire, and gun. . . . Management is their purposeful and continuing alignment."
> —Aldo Leopold, *Game Management*

Whether or not I can discern what the landowners have been up to with tools on their land, there are surprises and pleasures in a solitary excursion, even if brief, on well-cared for and much-loved private land. When that land has passed from one generation to another, what you see or smell or hear on a walk can suggest some of the family history written on the land: small orchards that are legacies of great-grandparents' commitments to better food; a patch of forest with native wildflowers brightening the carpet of the forest floor because an aunt loved their colors; or a long ago and still fenced-off portion of a marsh that keeps its nesting snipe, because the livestock are well managed.

While a walk may reveal how the owners have interacted with the land, a casual inspection is not likely to reveal much about the actual practices, devices, and methods. If we knew about choices of land-use practices and how the available tools were actually used, we would know much of what each generation's land stewards hoped to achieve. And then we might begin to surmise something about the difficult and increasingly complex choices that will be thrust onto subsequent generations. But that can only happen if the generation now leading the way on their land can inspire, choose wisely, and, in the tough times, persist.

Similar to the countless landowners that Sand County Foundation has had the privilege to interact with, we at the Foundation have a long-term view in the careful monitoring and managing of our own crop, forest, marsh, and savanna land along the sandy banks of the Wisconsin River in Wisconsin. For more than forty years, the Foundation has lit a candle to brighten an important corner of the stage of private landowner conservation challenges and opportunities. We have done so at the Leopold Memorial Reserve, where Aldo Leopold was inspired by his own land. The Leopold Conservation Awards program, begun and operated by Sand County Foundation, is our way of switching on the spotlights and turning up the voltage to showcase successful landowner conservation achievement. With the Leopold Conservation Awards, Sand County Foundation and its agricultural and conservation partners show how families have produced gratifying results by taking individual responsibility and actively addressing their place in civil society. These— and many other landowners—are living a land ethic in accord with Aldo

Leopold's writings about his own land management and monitoring work in the 1930s.

First widely read in the 1970s, Leopold's writings have been celebrated ever since. Because of him, thousands of people have been inspired to make better decisions about their own contributions to better land health. In the face of increasing land subdivision, greater tax burdens, a complicated regulatory environment, and ever more challenging economics, we established the Leopold Conservation Award as a testament to Leopold's expression of hope translated into twenty-first-century private landowner conservation achievement. This book features families that own and manage land. Their lands—productive working lands—are a credit to themselves, their communities, and this nation. These families make management decisions and choose appropriate tools based as much on inspiration and grit as on a balance sheet or cash flow projection.

The Leopold Conservation Award winners featured here are not alone. They join hundreds of other private landowners whose working lands show that responsible, cost-effective conservation outcomes can be earned, but probably not bought. Simply put, the Leopold Conservation Awards show that remarkable people in the United States of America still do remarkable things on their land—with great benefits for the rest of us. Even though successful twenty-first-century landowners may use different tools, they still, like Leopold, wake up in the morning with a commitment to do better things on their land; they know that a community of people and other species rely on the impact of their commitments. And, if they are like Aldo Leopold in another respect, they will take an occasional long ramble before breakfast and be enlightened by what they hear and see of their neighbors, both human and non-human.

Whether on healthy land or abused land, a quick visit, a short walk, and several hasty glances might be good for speculation's sake and could whet one's intellectual curiosity. However, when it comes down to really comprehending landowners' commitment and capability on the land, including what "tools" they choose to use and how well they deploy them,

Sand County Foundation and its partners count on discerning people who know more and have been accumulating knowledge over a much longer period of time than a single morning's stroll.

The Leopold Conservation Award program recognizes landowners actively committed to living the Leopold legacy. We view the Leopold Conservation Awards as important investments in private lands conservation. To ensure the best value from those investments, we rely on advisor partners who provide nominations and evaluate each state's contenders. Those who nominate and those who evaluate are the discerning people whose judgment we rely upon.

While our Leopold Conservation Award winners are certainly accomplished, none of them are successful by virtue of following a script or a game plan. These people are creative and inventive; they remain on their land amidst tumultuous economic and social circumstances. Aldo Leopold recognized and celebrated the creativity that often accompanied necessity among landowners.

> Acts of creation are ordinarily reserved for gods and poets, but humbler folk may circumvent this restriction if they know how. To plant a pine, for example, one need be neither god nor poet; one need only own a shovel. By virtue of this curious loophole in the rules, any clodhopper may say: Let there be a tree—and there will be one. If his back be strong and his shovel sharp, there may eventually be ten thousand. And in the seventh year he may lean upon his shovel, and look upon his trees, and find them good.
> —Aldo Leopold, *A Sand County Almanac*

The revelations in this book about remarkable, creative people on healthy land are from the pen of a talented writer, Joe Nick Patoski. He spent considerable time with each family, as well as with the partners and neighbors who nominated the families for Leopold Conservation Awards. From these members of the landowners' communities, he developed a good idea of which "tools" are used to effect improved land health and which have helped to keep good people on good land without spoiling it—one of the greatest, never-ending challenges to humankind.

The landowners in this book have improved their land and done so by being profitable, generous to their human community, committed to family, and desirous of leaving land better than it was when it came into their stewardship. The "tools" these landowners use are often similar to the "axe, cow, plow, fire, and gun" of Leopold's time, but they also use other "tools" like educational ranch tours, volunteer leadership within local government, and deliberate and documented testing of innovations in management.

We could not reference the Leopold Conservation Awards and our pride in having launched this private landowner recognition program without tying this book and its stories to selections from Aldo Leopold's writings. As I close this foreword, I can do no better than to share a few lines from "The Land Ethic" found near the very end of Leopold's *A Sand County Almanac*:

> An innumerable host of actions and attitudes, comprising perhaps the bulk of all land relations, is determined by the land-users' tastes and predilections, rather than by his purse. The bulk of all land relations hinges on investments of time, forethought, skill, and faith rather than on investments of cash. As a land-user thinketh, so is he.

If you are a person whose imagination can run a little wild while on a morning's walk across someone else's land-ownership, you will very likely find these *Generations on the Land* families' "investments" of spirit, intellect, and muscle to be as inspiring as I do.

—Brent M. Haglund
President, Sand County Foundation

Generations on the Land

Michelle, Bret, Laura, and Fred Selman (Photo by Ron Francis)

CHAPTER 1

Harold Selman Ranches

Every day in rural America, farmers and ranchers get up from their beds and go out to do their work on the land. In twenty-six years working with the Natural Resources Conservation Service, I have never met a landowner who got up in the morning and said, "I am headed out to destroy my land." Most landowners manage based on what they know.

In every resource professional's life, a few very bright lights shine. Those bright lights are the handful of ranchers and farmers who exemplify the best of the best in terms of their stewardship commitment. These landowners can't get enough resource knowledge; they think first of conservation because they realize that their stewardship will sustain the operation and its economic viability, not just during their lifetime but for future generations. The Natural Resources Conservation Service is proud to take part in honoring these outstanding landowners through the Leopold Conservation Award in the same way we take pride in a wide array of cost-share programs that assist them in fulfilling their vision for enhancing the natural resources in their care.

I have been blessed to work with many of these amazing people. Two of the most outstanding are Fred and Laura Selman. This couple works tirelessly and with amazing enthusiasm, forging partnerships that bring them the knowledge and assistance they need to ensure the health of their land. I have watched them creatively unite environmental and production interests to protect their land from development. They bring resource professionals with divergent interests together to come up with the best ideas for applied management. Both Fred and Laura give generously of their time to transfer information to other landowners through involvement with the Box Elder County Conservation District. They are both very active with the Utah Wool Growers and Utah Cattlemen's Association education efforts. They are amazing people who add value to the land, their community, and to all who come in contact with them. It has been my privilege to help them in some small way.

—Sylvia Gillen
Utah State Conservationist,
Natural Resources Conservation Service

Selman Ranch (Photo by Ron Francis)

You can never know too much. There's always something new to learn. That is the guiding philosophy of Harold Selman Inc., the sheep ranches currently run by Fred Selman (Harold's son) and his family in the Bear River Valley of northern Utah. Straddling Cache and Box Elder counties, this swath of land in the foothills of the Wasatch Mountains is the most ag-intensive part of the state or as Laura Selman (Fred's wife) more eloquently put it, "the last of the good, green space in Utah."

Numerous outside pressures have threatened their way of life, including land fragmentation and creeping urbanization, but the Selmans aren't sweating. They've practiced exemplary stewardship of the land they love and over the years have grown to better understand the power of education and engagement and the differences they can make when dealing with outside interests. Even in the rush to prepare for shipping lambs that marked the end of summer and the beginning of autumn, they took time to stop, pause, and listen to what folks had to say. On this particular Saturday, a lady from nearby Logan stopped by the house after she'd been to the Selmans' pick-your-own garden, which was ripe with melons, squash, corn, potatoes, peppers, and pumpkins. She informed the Selmans that the tomatoes she had just picked from their field were "the plumpest, juiciest, most beautiful tomatoes I've seen in years!"—which explains why some of the Selmans' pick-your-own customers drive all the way from Wyoming, Idaho, and Nevada.

Fred and Laura's son, Bret Selman, 41, likes to tell the story of a conversation with an environmentalist as an example of how talking and listening made a difference. The two were serving on a national forest planning committee. The fellow had confronted Bret about the Selmans' grazing sheep in a designated wilderness area. "I have a real problem with that," he told Bret. "Why don't you take your sheep and go somewhere else? What do you need to be there for?"

Over the course of an hour's worth of civil conversation, Bret laid out the consequences of the gentleman getting his wish.

Bret explained the whole operation, detailing the annual movement from the desert to lambing grounds to spring range and the summer wilderness range where the sheep got fat on the premium, high-mountain grasses. "You take that away, that takes away our sheep operation," Bret told him. "There's nowhere to go. I'm not going to starve. What would you have me do? Do you want me to sell ranchettes on our private ground, and get rid of the wildlife winter range where the deer and the elk have their young? Do you want me to sell that for houses, put blacktop on it and strip malls?"

By the end of the visit, the man had come around. "I've been fighting against you my entire life," he told Bret, "when I should have been fighting for you."

It goes both ways. Bret related how he used to consider "jack snipes" to be varmints that puddled in the hay the family was trying to get established, until it was pointed out to him by a biologist that the "jack snipe" was a white-faced ibis on the sensitive species list—and that some of the largest numbers of the species found in Utah were on their land.

Similarly, when Bret complained that the windbreak of squaw bush, locust, and evergreens he and his father had planted wasn't attracting pheasant coveys, one of Bret's tree-hugging friends, biologist Eve Davies, asked if there were magpie nests in the windbreaks because the notorious nest predator keeps out other birds, including pheasants.

"It was like somebody shot me with a rifle," Bret exclaimed dramatically with a goofy grin. "How stupid could I be? It was simple as that. I can get in the car with Eve and we're looking at the same scenery. But she's looking for things she's wired for, and I'm looking for things I'm wired for. When those two perspectives intermingle, that's when you learn."

His sons, Cole, 19, and Wyatt, 12, had been doing most of the teaching lately, Bret allowed. "When Cole can't identify a raptor, he'll look it up, and then he'll teach me. I'm the one supposed to be teaching him, but no sir, he's the one teaching me. Different interests bring out different things." Wyatt has a keen interest in noxious weeds, bugs, reptiles, and bio-control. He once spent an afternoon observing a praying mantis devouring a wasp and took photographs to demonstrate how the presence of the former reduces the population of the latter. Now Bret releases praying mantis eggs every spring around gates where wasps tend to congregate.

Bret admitted there are some issues that ranchers and environmentalists won't "ever be on the same page about," citing the practice of shooting coyotes as a means of predator control. "All they have to do is bring up wolves to make the hair on the back of my neck stand up," he said; the Selmans have yet to come around to seeing wolves and coyotes as anything other than threats to their livestock. "We just don't go there." Instead, when in the "mixed company" of ranchers and environmentalists, Bret likes to find common ground on subjects everyone can agree on.

Bret's granddaddy, Harold Selman, was like that.

Harold, like his father John before him, was a sheep raiser. John Selman left England in the 1860s for Utah where he worked on sheep ranches, trailing sheep across the American West. After marrying, he settled on a farm in Ogden and raised vegetables and fruit. But raising sheep was his true passion. John and son Harold went into the sheep business together about 1918 and moved to the Bear River Valley, settling on an irrigated farm and running sheep. Harold spent most of his time with the sheep, while John stayed on the farm. But the Great Depression hit hard, and they lost their herd. But Harold never gave up hope. Along with his wife, Dorthella, and a nephew, Bill Goring, he confidently turned around and bought another herd of sheep a few years later. Dorthella had saved a little money, and she willingly invested it in purchasing the herd, giving her a vested interest in the family business. In 1944, they purchased the ranch near Tremonton where the Selmans live today.

Harold brought with him a desire to leave the land better than he found it. He understood the cycle of grazing, how the practice could actually improve the land, and how it could harm it irreparably. Harold got a reputation for his ability to get sheep men and cow men to sit down and talk. Even though Harold didn't drink, he sometimes brought along a bottle of whiskey to ease the way between the two historically contentious parties. An abiding conservation ethic led him to voluntarily cut his stock numbers grazing on federal lands in Logan Canyon in the 1960s; he was the first rancher in the county to do so.

Fred recalled that his "dad sat on the [BLM] grazing board ever since I was a little kid. . . . He had a chance to inject a lot of ideas. . . . We understood the West was overgrazed. . . . Those were hard times back in the '20s, '30s and '40s. That's where my dad was vocal: how can we cut our numbers, still stay in existence, and raise better quality?"

For Harold, the light went on when President Franklin D. Roosevelt signed the Taylor Grazing Act of 1934. The act held liable every individual party that held a federal grazing permit. Before the act was signed,

Sharp-tailed grouse at Selman Ranch (Photo by Ron Francis)

stockraisers could graze public lands to the point of destroying grasses—if they could get to a patch of prime pasture before other grazing permit holders did.

Fred's own "Eureka! moment" came in the 1970s when environmental advocates raised red flags about ranchers poisoning coyotes as a means of predator control. "It was a hot issue," he admitted:

> I said, "You know, we don't think we're that bad a people. We do a lot of things not only for our private lands, but for permits where we work. We oughta start carrying a camera and take pictures of things we do that [are] environmental friendly." [So] we did that,

showing where we planted a windbreak, our pond development on our land and on national forest land, for our livestock and for wildlife. We've got one permit in a non-motorized wilderness area and [it had] a livestock pond that had filled up with mud; it wasn't any good for anything. We wanted to clean it out and Bret took a team of horses and packed in a slip scraper on a packhorse and worked it over and made a nice watering facility. It wasn't long before the Forest Service noticed and said, 'Look what these guys have done.' You get a change of attitude. We've developed watering facilities on our private lands to get livestock out of the riparian area. We've spent a lot of labor and money doing these things.

Fred sat on the Northern Utah Conservation board for twenty-eight years, all the while continuing to look for ways to make the land better. He did this together with the rest of the Harold Selman, Inc. operation: Laura, his wife of fifty years; their son, Bret, and his wife, Michelle (a city girl who's been helpful in teaching the Selmans how to deal with city people), and their children, Cole, Elke, age 15, Wyatt, and Julia, age 7. Fred's brother Dean is also part of the team. He sold his share of the ranch, but continues to advise the family on sheep-raising strategies. Fred and Laura's other children, Jonie and Kristy, live within ten miles of the home ranch in the Bear River Valley; their families enjoy helping out at the ranch whenever needed.

Laura spent twenty-five years working for the U.S. Department of Agriculture's Farm Service Agency, and she represented family interests in many local and area organizations. Bret was the first rancher to sit on the board of the Bridgerland Audubon Society. The Selmans' high local profile is enhanced by their reputation for knowing how to put cattle and sheep on the same land and not overgraze. "It's a management science, no question," Fred said.

Theirs is a natural operation. They don't use steroids or stimulants of any kind, although if their sheep or cattle are sick, they know how to doctor them. "People want to know where their meat comes from, how it is raised, how it is fed," Laura said, acknowledging the growing health concerns of folks in the United States. "We want to know what goes through our bodies more than ever before."

By far the biggest learning experience the Selmans have had in recent years was in making the decision to place 6,700 acres of their ranch into a conservation easement to be purchased by The Nature Conservancy.

"I was kind of nervous about The Nature Conservancy," admitted Laura, a petite fireball of a lady. "We heard stories about them from ranchers around Cody, Wyoming, telling us how awful easements were and we shouldn't have anything to do with The Nature Conservancy. So we tried to find something wrong. What's wrong with them?"

Every question the Selmans raised was eventually met with an answer they liked. When there was a roadblock, the discussion backed up and started over. "It took five years to do it the way we wanted to do it," Laura recounted. "Everything we wanted, they were able to come up with a way to do it. Hopefully, they got everything they desired, also. It is probably the most positive thing we've done in our lives. That land we were trying to preserve is preserved forever, and we get to continue our farming and ranching operation without changing a thing. That's what we want for our family and our grandchildren."

Their home ranch of irrigated fields covers 360 acres, and they have access to 25,400 acres of private ground; they also have grazing permits in the national forest and on BLM lands, giving them more than enough land to run their herd of 2,500 Columbia ewes. They also raise 130 head of cattle (a Hereford-Angus-Shorthorn mix for what Fred called "that crossbred vigor").

Sheep outfits have traditionally been gypsy operations, and the Selmans are no different. They run their sheep into the high forest of Logan Canyon every July 5, where their stock can be constantly on the move, browsing the geraniums, columbine, protein-rich legumes, and forbs that burst forth during the short growing season at 9,000 feet. The sheep bed on different ground every night, herded by five hired Peruvian hounds. In early September, the sheep are brought off the Rough

Allotment in the National Forest. Toward the middle of September, lamb shipment begins; the ewes move to their fall grazing, and cattle graze the conservation easement lands.

The easement agreement brought in enough cash for the Selmans to purchase another 5,200 acres of high desert west of Tremonton, as well as the farm where Laura Selman was raised. The purchase provided the family with the first lambing grounds for their Columbia ewes that they'd ever owned. A five-mile pipeline and new, strategically placed water tanks will complete the chain. "We've got our summer permits and our winter grounds. Now we've got somewhere to lamb our sheep. Before this, we always had to lease a place."

The Selmans also have an association with the Audubon Society that began in the mid-1990s, when the family leased fall pastureland in the Logan Bottoms. It was then that they met Eve Davies, a biologist for Rocky Mountain Power. "She was kind of a tree-hugger gal," said Bret, cracking a smile as he recalled their first encounter. "She said she couldn't get along with ranchers. I told her she could get along with me. 'Whatever you say, we'll do.'" A friendship formed. When Bret took her out on family land and they observed thirty-five sharp-tailed grouse dancing in the field one morning, the Selmans found an advocate and an entrée into the Audubon Society.

On the last Saturday morning of April every year, the Selmans host more than one hundred birding enthusiasts from as far away as Japan for what the family calls "Birdy Day." In addition to seeing rare birds, the crowd gets to enjoy a breakfast of lamb sausage, potatoes, and eggs prepared by the family. "We love having people on the ranch," Laura said. "We have some beautiful birds here." With the help of birders and biologists, they've identified twelve threatened species on one of their ranches.

Their birding friends became impassioned defenders, speaking on the Selmans' behalf when Cache and Box Elder counties attempted to authorize motorized vehicles to cross the Selmans' property for access to a four-wheeler loop.

"Private property is important to us," Laura said. "We don't have a problem with people seeing it, being on it, but we do not want motorized vehicles destroying it. This land isn't ours. We're just stewards of it. We're not taking it with us, so let's make it better. If we don't take care of this stuff, it's not going to be here.

"But we're still learning," Laura Selman said emphatically, nodding toward her husband. "We don't say we have the answers. We want to see if there's something better than [what] we're doing."

So, few people around Tremonton were surprised when word started floating about that a theory developed by Bret and Fred had drawn academic attention. Mountain mahogany—a critical, nutrient-packed winter food for local mule deer—was failing to regenerate across Utah. But Bret had noticed one place where there were numerous mahogany saplings and seedlings: on the trail up the ridge of Logan Canyon, where every July he pushed 1,000 ewes and their lambs seven miles to dine on Forest Service grasses. "It's the only place I've observed mahogany regenerating," he said. Could hoof action disturbing the seedbed in the sandy soil have had an impact? The Selmans alerted researchers, and at least one graduate student is interested in writing a master's thesis on the topic. As tended to happen when the Selmans were involved, people recognized that there was something new to be learned.

Gary and Sue Price (Photo by Chase Fountain)

CHAPTER 2

77 Ranch

In Texas we are losing productive, open-space land faster than any other state in the nation. Our legendary wide-open spaces are becoming cluttered with suburbs, shopping malls, and miles and miles of asphalt. The landscape is literally changing before our eyes.

As a result, caring for the land and the resources is no longer enough. Today's most effective stewards must also be evangelists, spreading the good news of land stewardship to an ever-growing audience that has no relationship with the natural world.

Gary and Sue Price have embraced the challenge of communicating stewardship's message with the same zeal that they have embraced the challenge of managing the native Blackland Prairie that is the core of their 77 Ranch. On the ranch, they have succeeded by carefully observing the world around them, working with the natural forces that are in play, and moving deliberately toward the future. It is with their eyes on the future that they have opened their ranch gates and welcomed fleets of yellow school buses to the 77 Ranch, so children can experience life beyond the artificial habitats of concrete and carpet grass.

As Gary notes, "If we don't get kids on the land and make some connection, there will be consequences. You never know when it's going to turn a kid on, where he or she sees something they're exposed to and it turns their head

*around." Of course, their hospitality and their outreach are extended to adults
as well, with equally positive results.*

*Turning heads and turning hearts is stewardship on a grand scale, making
the Prices influential far beyond their fence lines.*

—David K. Langford,
Vice President Emeritus, Texas Wildlife Association

Bluebonnets at 77 Ranch (Photo by Chase Fountain)

G ary Price will be the first to tell you that family is what you make of it. Blood runs thick, but in his own case, the deeper connection between people comes through the land. Gary and Sue Price's 77 Ranch is a shining example of that. On the rolling plains of Navarro County in north Central Texas forty miles south of Dallas, the ranch is a mosaic of native prairie that has never seen a plow and land that had been plowed until the soil wore out—making it property prime for rehabilitation. The Prices run their operation with an eye on how nature worked before the land had been farmed. Following that principle has allowed Gary and Sue to make a good living. Most of all, though, the 77 is a testament to Lee Low, the man who established the ranch decades before the Prices bought it. Although he passed away in 1987, Lee Low remains a constant in their lives, from his portrait hanging on the wall of their living room to the name of their son—Gary Lee—to their reputation around the community of Blooming Grove as progressive cattle ranchers with an encyclopedic knowledge of native grasses. Lee Low conveyed that rare sense of stewardship that wedded economics to environment. The Prices embraced his philosophy and have since taken it to the next level.

Lee was not related to Gary, who was raised in the nearby town of DeSoto. But he just as well could have been. Ever since the day Gary's parents brought their eight-year-old son to meet the man partial to overalls and a rumpled hat, and he mounted Gary on a horse named Budweiser, Gary grew up under Lee Low's influence. He hunted, fished, and rambled around the 77 Ranch with Lee and did plenty of exploring on his own. In the process, he learned a lot about ranching and about life.

"That guy up on the wall is my mentor," Gary said, fixing his deep-set eyes on the oil portrait of Low by the fireplace. "We spent a lot of time together on horseback. We rode together, worked cattle together, and were very, very close. He taught me to ranch looking down the line twenty years from now."

Lee Low was raised in the arid plains near San Saba, one hundred miles west of Blooming Grove. He began ranching in Navarro County in 1922, bringing some of the first Brahman cattle into the area. He practiced intensive rotational grazing, an efficient, effective method of grazing cattle, in the 1940s, long before it was embraced on a large scale by other ranchers.

"Lee taught me leaving grass was not really wasting it," Gary said. "You didn't have to run it through a cow." He fully understood the role of grasses in holding water and enriching the soil, and worked to prevent runoff. "I've seen Lee Low cut a tree, drag it with a horse, to put it across a cow trail that's eroding the land and starting a wash," Gary recalled. "There's more to ranching than short-term gains."

Their relationship inspired Gary to earn a degree in animal science at Texas A&M and manage a ranch in North Texas after graduating. He was working for a veterinary pharmaceutical company out of Lubbock when he met Sue, who'd developed her own deep love of the land on visits to her grandparents' 100-acre farm near the town of Eula.

Gary and Sue married in 1977, the same year Lee Low decided it was time to let go of the 77. His only son had passed away, and there was no one to inherit the ranch. So he approached the newlyweds, offering to sell them the 272-acre core of the ranch. Lee Low knew if he had to let go of the land he loved so dearly, it would be in good hands with the young man he'd watch grow up.

"For him to come up with this idea, just changed everything," Gary said, still a little in awe over how things worked out. He convinced the veterinary pharmaceutical company to transfer him to north Central Texas in 1978 so he could fall back on his day job if ranching was a bust. After Gary Lee was born in 1979, Sue began teaching elementary school in the nearby community of Blooming Grove.

In 1987, the year Lee Low passed away, Gary quit the veterinary pharmaceutical job to run the ranch full time. Slowly but steadily, Gary and Sue built up their operation, growing the ranch to 2,000 acres.

"We got more opportunities, started running more cattle, and bought more land when neighbors put theirs up for sale," Gary said. The whole venture was a long-odds proposition. "There was a lot of debt, wondering how cow prices are going to make this work, but absolutely, we've done it. Everything's come off the land or that schoolhouse [where Sue worked for twenty-eight years] up there," he said.

Gary Lee was raised on the ranch and grew up to graduate from Texas A&M with an animal science degree; he went on to manage a larger spread near Matador in West Texas. But he still returns to the 77 to lend a hand whenever needed. An empty nest has hardly slowed down his parents, evidenced by the sling around Gary's neck protecting a broken shoulder. "A colt bucked me off. I shouldn't have been on him," he said sheepishly. There are always plenty of challenges to face. "We don't have any other source of income," Gary said. "We have to get this right. We make a lot of land payments and a lot of interest to go with that. There's no oil production. This has got to be right." Especially when Mother Nature isn't cooperating.

"We've been through hard times with the [four-year] drought, selling calves for twenty-seven cents a pound, and dealing with price volatility," Gary said. "We're in good shape, but trying to predict where things are headed is impossible. There's been a drought in 2000, 2005, 6, and 7. Thirty tanks are completely dry. They've never been dry. Trying to restock cattle at prices we know are inflated is a challenge when you're trying to balance all that out with the grasses. We have to wean cattle in the fall, but we can't be buying grain like we have in the past. We're going to have to be more forward thinking in what we do. I'll have to wean my calves longer and turn them out on grass. That means more room for yearlings plus cows."

Gary and Sue managed the ranch anticipating times like these. Relying on grasses rather than feed for their cattle made skyrocketing fuel costs and the inflation that went with them easier to endure. "People are more open to change when fertilizer is going to $800 a ton. We can't keep spending money for fertilizer like that," Gary observed. "You can't ranch behind a John Deere. You've got to quit beating yourself over the head, trying to kill what's trying to grow there. Then the big picture begins to make more sense."

The Prices ran Hereford-Brahman crosses, F1-type cows, but were moving toward a smaller Brangus-Baldy-type cow for efficiency. "You don't need a 1,400 pound cow out there," Gary said. "We do want a little Brahma influence, we're not that wedded to just straight Angus. You've got to fit the cow to the environment. We may give up a little in production, but we'll gain it back with value and by being all-natural."

To achieve those goals, the Prices believe, ranchers need to stop, look, and listen to the land, and pay special attention to what was there before, keeping in mind that what might appear to be a weed could be a beneficial plant. The prairie that existed before Navarro County was settled functioned fairly efficiently. "Lots of ranchers have been locked into these high-intensity systems that require a lot of input and now they're scratching their heads asking, 'Where do we go from here?' We've already gone to a slower pace, so we're OK, moving forward with all this. It allows you to stay when your competition has to go. When markets are bad, you're able to hold on. We still have questions about what's going to happen, but we've built a system we've been working on a long time, trying to find that optimum balance."

The 77 ranch is on the Blackland Prairie, once part of a region of lush tallgrass prairies that stretched from Manitoba in western Canada to the Texas coast. But the nutrients in the rich mix of sandy loam and black river bottom dirt were depleted by the early twentieth century, when more cotton was farmed in neighboring Ellis County (which includes a small piece of the 77) than any county in the United States.

"Every acre around here that could be farmed for cotton was put into production until it was worn out," Gary said. "I understand that. It was the Great Depression and people were trying to make a living any way they could." Many farmers walked away from their fields, and prickly pear, mesquite, and thorny locust thickets moved in, robbing grasses of water and what little nutrients were left, exacerbating soil erosion, and effectively destroying the ecological equilibrium of the once-bountiful prairie.

The lanky, soft-spoken Price knew that past well enough to deliver the good news: there were plenty of native grass seeds still in that soil—prairie remnants—and all they needed was a little hoof action at the right time and some rain to recover. Cows that grazed land in large numbers over short periods of time mimicked the intense pounding of prairie soil by migrating buffalos that aerated and opened up the soil. Any success the Prices had realized as ranchers could be traced to native grasses, and they managed them like trees. "You need to build the root system so it lasts longer. You've got to get the process started, and you'll hold more water."

With water and cattle, good native grasses make almost anything possible. Proof is the lush appearance of the 77 Ranch. Despite an extended drought and a torrid July heat wave, some seasonal creeks still held water. Considerable study and patience was required to get it right. Partnerships with numerous agencies proved invaluable. The U.S. Department of Agriculture and its Natural Resources Conservation Service, Texas AgriLife Extension, the Grazing Lands Conservation Initiative, Bluebonnet Resources Corporation, the Blooming Grove Future Farmers of America, and the Tarrant Regional Water District were all contributors to a 20-acre roadside demonstration project on the 77 in 1999.

The Prices' constant battle with invasive grass and woody plant species has been waged by burning and dozing, then aggressively planting native Eastern gamagrass propagules, switchgrass, Indian grass, big bluestem, little bluestem, and sideoats grama grass, as well as Hubam and Madrid clover as cover crops. "Burning controls some brush while adding nutrients to the soil in a fairly cost-effective way," Gary explained.

Over the years, they've learned to rethink strategies when necessary. "We cleared the mesquite off of this," Gary said, nodding toward a sloping meadow, "planted native grasses, mainly Eastern gamagrass. It's done real well, but we've realized it's not an upland grass—it's better suited for the bottoms."

Restoration included replacing historic plantings of KR bluestem grass, a hybrid developed for the King Ranch as a quick-growing cover, and coastal bermudagrass. Both hybrids have been popular with local farmers over the past sixty years, so Gary had to explain to his neighbors why he wanted to get rid of it. "KR was given to people to cover the bare ground" as a means of slowing runoff, he said. But KR was a monoculture with implications. "In this blackland, [biologists] think KR puts out an allelopathic effect, sending out a chemical barrier around it to keep other seed from germinating. That causes more soil erosion, creating more bare ground."

The Prices regard cultivation of coastal hay as "mining nutrients," a short-term success that will eventually deplete the soil. That action and reaction made long-term decision making critical. "If you don't know where you're going, any road will get you there," Gary said.

Bluebonnets at 77 Ranch (Photo by Chase Fountain)

KR and coastal bermudagrass also contributed to the loss of suitable habitat for bobwhite quail; their numbers declined in the mid-twentieth century after farmers began planting the hybrid grasses that pushed out the native tall grasses that were prime bobwhite habitat. As use of the hybrid grasses spread, quail populations crashed. The Prices and neighboring ranchers, who depended on hunting leases as part of their income, responded with the Western Navarro Bobwhite Restoration Initiative, bringing together interested landowners controlling 30,000 acres to work together to restore bobwhite habitat. As a result, reintroduction of native forbs and grasses has become a priority. Results came quickly. Despite extended drought, in 2008 quail numbers on the 77 Ranch were the highest in fifteen years.

"Some of it is as simple as starting with these grasses, letting landowners know quail can't nest in bermudagrass," Gary said. "Bobwhite can't use bermudagrass. They need bundleflower, ragweed, or sunflower"— weeds that farmers usually spray to keep out of their fields. That explains the reaction of some neighbors to the Prices' "weed" cultivation. "Most people would come through here and say 'You can't let this happen, you can't let that ironweed grow over there like that because it's going to spread. It's unkempt if you've got sunflowers back there. Call Dow. Start spraying.'"

He'd heard it all. "You have to understand, weeds are just a symptom of something else that may be wrong. You can put band-aids on it all you want, spending money to do that, but until you address the problem— which is usually bare ground, continuous overgrazing—you're not going to cure it. You're just going to beat yourself silly. If you're doing the right things for wildlife, it's going to be the right thing for cattle. We could plow this up and put it into Tifton 85, fertilize it, make it a monoculture that would look pretty to a lot of people, like a park, but you're shut down [from cattle raising] at $1,000 a ton fertilizer."

Paying attention to how a prairie functions as an ecosystem has led to a more cost-effective operation. "Sustainable cattle raising is based on cheap grass," explained Gary. "That leads to good water and soil composition—all those things are compatible with wildlife. I'm interested in what wants to grow here, and how I can use that instead of me manipulating the vision. There's so much we don't know about microorganisms and about sterilizing the ground with chemicals, such as the impact of dung beetles on breaking down manure and improving the nitrogen cycle."

As he toured the ranch in his pickup truck, Gary explained the patchwork of property; there are thirty different pastures that two herds of cattle are rotated through. "Even though this is in good condition, it's still going to be behind. . . . This was plowed. . . . This is probably the way it looked 200 years ago . . . and there's some KR."

Pointing out some particularly hardscrabble land, he said, "The good soil there is in the Gulf of Mexico." Poor management showed. More hooves on the soil would eventually begin to remediate the land. "One of the biggest challenges we've had lately is not having enough cattle to really hammer the soil with intensive grazing, but you have to balance that out with economics. . . . If you don't, you're making a big mistake with tunnel vision."

Slow was better, and it wasn't just in the way Gary drawled or what Lee Low taught him. It was the best way to understand the land. "To get a feel for this place, I want to watch, I want to listen. Watch how a cow grazes pasture. They take a bite and walk on. You've got to watch that third or fourth bite, though," he smiled confidently. If "you're harvesting the leaves, you better leave something there that goes into the roots. Some native grasses we know are eighty years old, as old as a tree, so you manage it like a tree. You take the fruit off of it, but you don't want to take too much, 'cause you've got to build a root system to withstand drought like we're in now. When it quits raining, we know we have to have these tall grasses for nesting quail and turkey."

"Slow" drives Sue and Gary's whole way of thinking about ranching. "It's about staying here and doing it another year," he said. "My ultimate goal is to stay on the land." One sure way to do so is better management of water. "Water is what's going to be driving the development of Texas," Gary acknowledged. "We understand water here. Ranching, you understand that you can't make it rain. It's the limiting factor of ranching. You can't control how much water you get, but you certainly can control how much water you keep. Urban folks need to have that same consciousness, to conserve as much as you can."

The Prices tried to do their part by sculpting the drainage above Mill Creek to better filter runoff with grasses. If and when it ever rained again, they'd be ready. Earth had been dammed for a 10-acre lake and a 40-acre wetland nearby (a project Ducks Unlimited helped underwrite).

The decision to devote that land to water management meant giving up revenue from the farmer who had been leasing the land to grow corn (200 acres of the 77 was being farmed for corn, milo, and cotton). "But the erosion was so bad, you could put a truck in it," he said. "We could lose twenty acres in a heavy rain. So we rebuilt the levees and we'll be flooding this cornfield after the crop is out."

"[Allan] Savory says it's about harvesting sunlight," Gary said. "That's what we do. We harvest water, we harvest sunlight, put it in a saleable form." "Exhibit A" is Mill Creek, about two miles from the house, which feeds Chambers Creek and eventually drains into the Trinity River. Chambers Creek is one of the main contributors to the Richland Chambers Reservoir, which pumps water to the western half of the sprawling Dallas-Fort Worth metro area. "There's a real connection," Gary explained matter-of-factly. "The water that goes over our land ends up as drinking water in the Metroplex." Cleaner water going into the reservoir means less money spent to treat it.

For that and other reasons, the Prices devote considerable time to bringing biologists, researchers, and especially students to the ranch through programs with the Texas Wildlife Association's private land-owners' organization and Texas Parks and Wildlife. "If we don't get kids on the land and make some connection, there will be consequences," Gary warned, speaking from experience. "You never know when it's going to turn a kid on, where he or she sees something they're exposed to and it turns their head around."

In 2007, Sue Price rounded up the fourth grade class at Blooming Grove Elementary and fourth graders from St. John's in Dallas to do a dual six-week science study; they tested the water at White Rock Lake in Dallas and in Mill Creek and visited Texas Parks and Wildlife's Texas Freshwater Fisheries Center in Athens.

"They found there's very little pollution in this Mill Creek watershed," said Sue. "That was the best field trip I've ever had in my twenty-eight years of teaching." The experience led Gary and Sue to realize local students were no more educated about land issues than the city kids. "There's a lot to be done in educating rural areas as well," Sue said. "The longer and deeper we've gotten into this, the more we realize how little we really know. There's nothing like the land to humble you. Like now, when the grass doesn't grow, with this heat wave and drought."

"It's an ongoing process. We're feeling our way through it," Gary said. "But one of the things they think may come from this will be . . . monitoring devices down on the creek, in the watershed to do some real-time monitoring for classrooms. You could track a rain event."

The Prices have improved the 77 Ranch to the point where they could sell out and live comfortably for the rest of their lives. But that wouldn't be them. "The deed says we own it, but we really just lease it because we are only just passing through during our lifetime," Gary said, putting their role in perspective. "We have an obligation to be good stewards of what we have control over, just as we have an obligation with those people whose path crosses ours, to share that knowledge. We've been blessed."

When the time comes to pass along the 77, Gary Lee will get the first call. Gary Lee has been managing a much larger cattle ranch out in West Texas (his version of going to graduate school), but has already invested some of his savings in buying a couple hundred acres adjacent to the 77, which he is leasing to a farmer. Soon enough, he'd be going all in and doing it the right way, just like his folks—and just like Lee Low before them.

Charlie, Jaclyn, and Blaine Wilson (Photo by Bill Gillette)

CHAPTER 3

Wilson Ranch

The Sandhills of Nebraska have been described by many environment experts as one of the most fragile landscapes in the world. "Majestic" would be the term of choice by inhabitants of the area. Covered in a literal sea of grass, the Sandhills roll in waves for hundreds of miles covering one of the largest underground aquifers in the world. This unique blend of natural resources provides great opportunity for both wonder and devastation.

Ranch families like the Wilsons have been captivated by the wonder of the Sandhills. Their experience, patience, and persistence complement the rich land in creating a fantastic display of natural resource management. Jaclyn Wilson, while not the traditional image of the John Wayne cowboy, follows the true form of innovator. Ms. Wilson made a hard decision to return home, yet it is her un-regretted decision that has and will benefit not only her family but the Sandhills as well.

As you will read in this chapter, the Wilsons have their own unique strategies for private land management with which they excel not only in business but also in conservation. Like their neighbors, they have learned that the best strategies are not ones of force, but rather those of synergy.

—Michael Kelsey, Executive Vice President,
Nebraska Cattlemen

Prairie at Wilson Ranch (Photo by Bill Gillette)

Sometime between Jaclyn Wilson telling me how she dumped a boyfriend, a hulking 250-pound lineman for the Nebraska Cornhuskers, for asking "the wrong question about cattle," (no, cows do not migrate and fences aren't there to keep them from moving south) and watching her gracefully steer her quarter horse Ed to herd bulls from one green pasture to an even greener one, the future of the Wilson Ranch came into focus.

If you ran into Jaclyn Wilson on the streets of New York, the vivacious blonde would neatly fit the "Type A" personality profile: sharp, assertive, highly motivated—a commanding presence to be reckoned with.

When you run into her on the 20,000-acre spread in the rolling Sandhills of western Nebraska that is home to the Wilsonred, their Red Angus hybrid cattle, she's simply another hard-working hand, the latest in a line of parents, grandparents, uncles, aunts, and cousins dedicated to making a living from this remarkable piece of earth.

To hear her parents, Blaine and Charlie, tell it, Jaclyn taking over the ranch was practically a given. She was on a horse at age two, riding off on her own by age four. By the time she was eight, she was doing range studies, identifying plants and grasses. As a teen, she represented the ranching lifestyle at Girls State and Girls Nation (a photograph of her with President Bill Clinton is displayed in her modular home down the road from ranch headquarters). More recently, she'd been part of agricultural delegations to Poland, Russia, the Ukraine, and Brazil.

Out of earshot of her parents, Jaclyn confided that sticking with the family ranch was a hard choice. She'd seen the bright lights of the big city ("Believe me, I know my way around a subway") and studied four years at the University of Nebraska. She had plenty of reasons to follow her brother, Brett, who stayed in Omaha with his new wife to pursue a career in banking. She knew too well that ranching was still considered a man's game; she'd experienced it through her involvement with cattlemen's groups and related organizations. Her political skills could have easily led to a job to Washington. "I was really focused on politics, and had aspirations of going to law school and being a lobbyist," she admitted. "My dream job at that time would have been lobbyist for the National Cattlemen's Beef Association."

But after coming home weekends, school vacations, and during the summer to help out and seeing what needed to be done, and seeing her parents' and her uncle's to-do lists get longer, she knew she had to go all in. "There are times you get burnt out, or frustrated," she acknowledged. "You had to grow up way too fast. About two years ago, I finally came to the conclusion: This is good. It's worth it." She had taken to heart her Uncle Bryan's advice that she didn't know it all, "so I don't think I hardly said anything my first two years," she said. Two years later, she had earned enough respect to be included in discussions. Her dad eased the way. "We'd be at seminars and somebody would ask him questions about what's going on and he'd ask me, 'Is that right, Jaclyn?' or 'Is there something else to add?' He deferred to me. So I always made sure I had the right answer."

For all of Jaclyn Wilson's honest complaints about the dearth of social opportunities in this sparsely populated corner of the state, she gladly accepted the responsibility as the first of her generation to carry on the Wilson family brand. "It's a lot of pressure," she admitted. "You don't want to be the generation that gives it all up. It was so ingrained. One hundred twenty years is a long tradition. You're expected to fall in line, even if it's never said that you have to. You just expect it of yourself."

Her grounding was informed by the piece of earth she was tethered to, where land and sky were boiled down to their respective essences, making for a very stark and very beautiful landscape. Sculpted by eons of wind erosion, the Sandhills' treeless, grassy plains roll in velvety folds like waves on an ocean over almost 300 miles of western Nebraska. Pocked with wetlands and playa lakes that feed the Ogallala Aquifer, most of this endless open range has never seen a plow, making the Sandhills a haven for wildlife and one of the most stunning landscapes in North America.

The land is less welcoming to humans. There aren't many folks residing in this isolated region for a reason. But those who have managed to endure the cycles of blizzards, droughts, grasshoppers, and endless wind in order to eke out a living have stories to tell, a few of which unfolded over the course of a Sunday afternoon when Jaclyn's great-aunt, Cheryl Wilkinson, visited from Scottsbluff. She swapped family stories with Jane Wilson, Jaclyn's grandmother and the matriarch of the Wilson family, recalling digging up fossils of bear, giant camels, mammoths and saber-toothed tigers, as well as caches of bones from the buffalo that Anthony and Sarah Wilson survived on when they homesteaded the ranch in 1888.

Cheryl and Jane talked about Old Jules, the promoter who lured pioneers (including their own family) to settle the Sandhills territory. The area was known by the natives as Niobrara country, although Indian presence in the Sandhills was minimal. Blaine Wilson said he'd always heard that nearby tribes considered the Sandhills hostile territory, too easy to get lost in, so they stayed out.

Cheryl recalled the ranch's second matriarch, Helen Wilson, who went back to her native France before returning to Nebraska in 1910. Cheryl also mentioned the creative streak that runs in the family (Cheryl is an accomplished landscape painter). After one family member brought horses from Texas, the Wilsons eventually settled on raising beef cattle. With a constant eye on improving their stock, they began purebred Hereford production in 1934; through crossbreeding, they made the Register of Merit list for their Polled Herefords. Red Angus bulls entered the mix in the late 1970s, followed by introduction of South Devon bulls in the 1980s which were crossed into Red Angus in the 1990s. The most recent genetic improvement is Wilsonreds, the family brand of high percentage Red Angus, bred for efficiency, consistency, and weight gain.

The Sunday afternoon discussion swung from the necessity of Wilson kids having to live during the week with families up in Rushville, fifty-six miles north, so they could go to high school, to the imminent closing of the nearest one-room schoolhouse, to the likes and dislikes of brothers Blaine and Bryan—Jane's sons—who run the ranch. Blaine was the rock who couldn't take a vacation because he worried too much about what needed to be done at home. Bryan was the geneticist who returned to the ranch after learning computing skills and moved all the family cattle records online. Blaine was all about getting the hay in. Bryan was the AI (artificial insemination) guy. Blaine lived in the family house with his wife, Charlie. Bryan lived over the hill in another shaded home with his wife, Debbie, daughter Julia, and sons Braydon and Bryant, a.k.a. Buster, a name that goes back several generations.

Sunday visiting forced the family to stop and take a breather. "My mother makes sure that no matter how hard we work, we try to take a day off for conversation, for shopping, for traveling, for doing something other than working," Jaclyn explained about the gatherings. Her father nodded in agreement, cracking a hint of a parental smile. "We were doing everything we could to slow her down," he said. "It worked for awhile."

Jaclyn's a good hand, really. If she wasn't, she wouldn't be on the ranch.

One summer day began long before sunrise, like most other days, when Jaclyn fueled up her all-terrain four-wheeler and hopped on, with her dog Jazz sitting snug behind her. The four-wheeler was a technological advance the Wilsons embraced. "Over time, we've found they're a lot more efficient, and they're easier on this sandy soil," Jaclyn said. "Somebody told me short-term planning on a ranch is ten years. We've been using four-wheelers longer than that, and there are some areas that used to be trail road where the grass is coming back. We hardly use the pickup in the pastures anymore."

With an early morning chill hanging in the air, her dance card was full. There was feeding to do, gates to check, salt blocks and fly control liquid to deliver, cattle to move, and cows to artificially inseminate. She began by showing off some ethanol byproduct that was being used to grow and fatten cattle. With corn and fuel prices skyrocketing, the Wilsons were constantly on the lookout for more economical feedstuff. Driving the ATV to a nearby pasture, she demonstrated how fly control had changed. A mix of diesel fuel and vehicle oil used to be the preferred liquid applied to large hanging cloth flaps that the cattle liked to rub their backs on. But the Wilsons had switched to an insecticide and mineral oil mix that was environmentally safer and much more economical. "The cows love these things and they'll tear the heck out of them," Jaclyn said of the new, rubber flaps.

Setting down a salt block, she scanned the pasture and explained the marking system of ear tags, tattoos, and brands. "We know where every single cow is, at any given time of the year, and her whole history," she said. "This cow here is O 69. She's got a purple ear tag which means she's a registered cow of Dad's. The O means she was born in 2000. Up at the top, this 336 was her dam's number. On the side is N W that stands for None Wider—that's the bull that she's out of. Also, she's got a notch in her right ear which also means she belongs to Dad. She'll have two tattoos in the notched ear and she also has a hot-iron brand. We can take that O 69, enter it on Bryan's computer, and it will give us every single bit of information about her: what are her breed percentages, how many calves she's had, how those calves have performed, what percent of her body weight she's weaning, what her body condition and udder score is—everything you want to know about that cow is there."

Documentation is a Wilson specialty. Jaclyn's grandfather, Melvin, better known as Bus, kept records on index cards. Jaclyn's Uncle Bryan uses a software program called Cow Sense. "From the time a calf is born, we'll have its birth weight, gender, when it'll be vaccinated, weaning weight, yearling weight. If it's a heifer or a bull, we will use all of that data to help us determine whether we'll keep it or not. If it's a steer, we will follow it all the way to harvest." The information is critical in maintaining the Red Angus stock. After Jaclyn finished her brief tutorial, the windless pasture was enveloped in absolute silence, save for the occasional moo or bawl of a calf.

After inspecting water tanks in two pastures, Jaclyn four-wheeled to the corral behind Bryan's house where she coaxed and separated heifers with the help of Bryan's boys, Braydon and Bryant, who helped open and shut gates, then lined up those in estrus where they would enter, single file, a trailer that was the mobile inseminator. Inside, Bryan, with Jaclyn's help, injected bull semen from a frozen straw into the uterus of each young cow. After being inseminated, each heifer was marked with a black streak of paint on their hindquarter and sent out to pasture. The AI process was messy and required brute physical strength and considerable patience to put up with the kicking and fussing. Bryan managed to artificially inseminate fifty heifers that day.

The AI was complemented by carcass tests conducted by Bryan, which involved tracking random breeding from herd sires and unproven bulls through their life to improve conception rates, sizing, and uniformity.

"We had three years of these," Bryan said. "They were all random bulls, random mating. I took the heaviest-weight cows and the lower-weight cows—it was at least 200 pounds difference. When you took the hard carcass weight of their offspring, there was only a one pound difference between these big cows and the small cows. That told us, 'Why have a big cow?' None are 100% Red Angus. We're still looking for the right balance. It works best in our deal to have a three-quarters Red Angus. That's where you come into your uniformity and the composition of your animal."

"If you ever figure out an ideal, you won't be in the cattle business," observed Jaclyn. "Everything has to change. The whole purpose of a hybrid is to take the best of one breed and cross it with another breed to get the best of both breeds. In our case, we think the Red Angus has a lot more to offer in our area. I think it's going to be a huge trend in the next decade." Her uncle made it all easier to figure out. "Computing," as Bryan liked to say, "is an efficient way for us to keep track of stuff. It's a bit of an art."

Following a couple hours of AI, Jaclyn steered her four-wheeler to the horse barn where she saddled up her horse, Handy Eddie Savage (Ed), to herd twenty-nine herd sires and one iconic Longhorn (a fiftieth birthday present from family members to Blaine) from one pasture through several others to reach new grazing ground. She took a break for lunch and then got back on the four-wheeler to herd 250 head of Wilsonreds from an old pasture to a new one. Eventually, she would make it over to the hayfield where her mother and father were raking and baling hay; she helped finish baling the pivot—an expensive endeavor, as two passes over the field with the giant $100,000 irrigation tool costs $4,000 in fuel alone.

With an average rainfall of fourteen inches a year, the Wilsons had to know their range plants and how to most efficiently conserve water. Old Bus used to say that in dry years where there wasn't grass anywhere else, there was grass in the Sandhills. All the fruit trees—apple, chokecherry, pear, cherry, peach, apricot—and the spruce, pine, oak, cedar, aspen, elm,

Herding cattle at Wilson Ranch (Photo by Bill Gillette)

willow, cottonwood and other species shading the main headquarters were planted by either Jane or Charlie. "For every one hundred trees we planted, maybe three would survive," Charlie said. The survival rate had improved with the installation of five drip systems that watered some 300 trees.

Jaclyn's younger brother, Brett, the oldest son who was heir apparent according to the traditional pecking order on the ranch, may return to the ranch someday to join forces with Jaclyn and Bryan's children, although his older sister thinks he doesn't have her passion about cattle. "He's great at building fence, and running the swather [harvesting machine]. Every family needs a banker though." Her cousins Braydon and Bryant, Bryan's boys, will likely embrace ranching when they grow into adults, judging from their cowboy hats and boots and their willingness to help out.

Jaclyn was ready to work with them all. "I've done so many leadership seminars and personality training sessions that I'd like to think I'm a good people reader. I know both dad and Bryan's strengths," she said. "Bryan is so intelligent, he thinks about something forever, from every angle imaginable. Dad avoids conflict at all cost. I've never seen him and Bryan get into an argument. Dad's never going to upset anyone intentionally. Everybody gets along so great. The problem with the industry and the operation we're involved in is you take your work home with you. You can't leave it at the office. If you have problems with someone you're working with, you're eating supper with them at their house."

Her generation may be steeped in heritage, but it will likely bring about new changes, as each generation adjusts and adapts. One difference was Jaclyn applying for the Leopold Conservation Award, which she learned about through the Nebraska Cattlemen. Seeking any kind of recognition was something her parents would have never done. "Blaine and I are very low key, to-ourselves people," insisted Charlie. "We don't want the publicity. We're very private people. We don't like our name out there. Our business is our business. We don't call the recognition a benefit. It makes us uncomfortable."

"If I asked them again," Jaclyn admitted, "they would have said no."

Still, her folks are OK with the changing of the guard.

"Jaclyn's really good at seeing through us," her mother said. "And that's an attribute. We all think things have to be done a certain way. She's usually right on the mark." Jaclyn's social networking with other cattle raisers and her participation in exchange programs keeps her up to speed on technology and innovation.

She has first-hand knowledge of wetlands restoration, pasture cover, erosion control, raising game birds, fish stocking, windmill and tank building, windbreak design, acquiring additional property, and how grazing impacted Sandhills grasslands. Taking care of the land, raising livestock, and making ends meet are simultaneous challenges, and Jaclyn appeared ready to take them on. But she wasn't about to ponder whatever problems loomed around the corner for too long. It was six in the evening. Although she had ridden well over fifty miles on her four-wheeler, loading and unloading feed and fuel, moving, herding, and inseminating stock, opening and closing gates, there was still work to be done. She apologized as she hurriedly headed out the door. She throttled up the four-wheeler, her dog Jazz hopped on back, and they sped off toward the sun dipping to the horizon.

Working hard is the only way to live.

Thomas, Kaye, Taylor, and Terry Peters (Photo by Jeff Peters)

CHAPTER 4

Terry Peters

The forests of Wisconsin have a long and rich history of multiple uses, providing environmental, economic, and social benefits to the people of the state. Wisconsin's landowners face many challenges. The greatest negative impact on forest biodiversity is permanent fragmentation—the long-term conversion of forestland to non-forest uses and loss of habitat. Additionally, the threat of uncontrolled invasive species has the potential to forever alter the forests as we know them today.

Terry Peters understands that actions we take today affect the forests of tomorrow. His vision and goals include sustainable management to ensure that the forests remain intact and managed for future generations. It is that practice and his advocacy for sustainable management that earned Terry the Leopold Conservation Award.

Terry starts at home by first setting goals and laying out management plans, then making sure everyone (family and crew) buys in and works toward the vision.

Terry doesn't stop with his own land or his own family. He shares the sustainable forestry message in many ways, including speaking at the Northern Great Lakes Visitor Center; participating on the advisory board and lecturing at the Sigurd Olson Environmental Institute at Northland College; being a charter member of the Bad River Watershed Association; supporting the Great

Lakes Timber Professionals Association; and proudly participating in the "Log A Load for Kids" charitable timber harvest.

Although woods work is serious business and sometimes the rewards are very small, Terry always has a positive attitude and a good word for anyone he meets. Even when a log truck went down a steep hill backwards on an icy woods road and tipped over, Terry's only reaction, after making sure no one was hurt, was to smile and say "Let's get 'er upright and back on the road, supper's waiting."

—Paul DeLong,
Wisconsin State Forester

Sun shining through the trees on Terry Peters's land (Photo by Kevin Kiley)

Terry Peters chose to start the tour where the product of his livelihood is on view—at North Country Lumber, the hardwood sawmill in Wisconsin's remote Northwoods where stacks of giant logs of hard maple, red oak, basswood, soft maple, birch, and oak were being sawed, shaped, and sanded into high-end wooden window frames, cabinets, and furniture destined for domestic and overseas markets. The sawmill is a high-tech operation, built thirty years ago and upgraded over the years with laser beams, automation, and technology that made use of every piece of wood involved in the saw-to-board process, down to the pulpwood chips and sawdust that fuel the furnaces, kilns, heaters, and engines on the mill site. The log procurement manager is Tim Lee, a cousin of Terry Peters. Many relatives, it seemed, are involved with the spunky 55-year-old who was giving me an informal seminar on the logging process in reverse, from transporting and processing, to stacking, to slashing and cutting.

Terry Peters and his family were born to log. From the felled white pine log on display in front of his office on the main drag of Mellen, Wisconsin to the "LOG A LOAD" vanity plates adorning the flex-fuel GMC Yukon XL he drove, Terry loves playing to stereotype. He dresses like a logger in boots, jeans, and Pendleton shirt, talks like a logger with a pinched, vaguely Nordic accent, lives like a logger deep in the woods, and finds time to proselytize on behalf of Wisconsin loggers and logging.

The family's roots run deep in the heavy loam of the Northwoods. Various Peters' and Larsons' from Norway and Sweden began settling this part of upper Wisconsin in 1888. Thomas Larson, Terry Peters's great-grandfather, opened a shoe shop in Mellen in 1900, before clearing portions of his land to farm full time in 1910 in order to "prove up" the 160 acres he had homesteaded. Like other farmers, Thomas logged in the winter when his fields were fallow, often leaving the farm for extended periods to live in lumber camps.

Thomas Larson's son-in-law, Herman Peters, farmed and logged, too, and he owned and operated a sawmill where his grandson, the very same Terry Peters I was talking to, played and worked as a boy. Herman's son (and Terry's father) was Howard "Bud" Peters; he was the first in the family to work full time as a timber harvester and sawmill operator.

Terry Peters had witnessed dramatic changes in silvaculture in the thirty-five years he had been working these woods. Logging used to be the dominant lifestyle of the region, defined by rugged men wielding axes, mythic characters such as Paul Bunyan, and sawmills around almost every bend of a river—each one ready to purchase as many logs as a lumberjack could deliver. But as wood processing evolved into a global industry, the wood workforce in Wisconsin and across the United

States declined rapidly. Hanging on in a business where the competition included Brazilian eucalyptus plantations owned by American paper companies, massive logging operations in New Zealand, and clear-cut operations in China, required creative thinking.

Terry owned 3,200 acres of woodlands and had tens of thousands more acres of leased forestland. He directed his loggers to be guided by a simple principle: "You only cut a certain amount. You leave enough value for us and for the songbirds. We're protecting our self-interest. Not every acre has to be harvested. It's not what you take out. It's what you leave behind. We've harvested all around Mellen and very few people know where we've logged."

The approach is part of Terry's concept of holistic logging. "Loggers have to know the barks of various species because the best time of the year to log is when the leaves have fallen," he said. Frozen ground was far easier to negotiate than the mud that comes with the spring thaw and rains. Summer logging doesn't really begin in earnest until July when the ground finally dries out, unless the spring rains keep coming. Unlike forests out west, these woods don't burn. "You can light as many matches as you want," he offered. "It's too wet here."

"Each hardwood has different properties and different times of the year for ideal cutting," Terry said, walking around the stacks of felled logs outside North Country Lumber. There was a three-month window toward the end of winter that was ideal for getting maple "off the stump" to best avoid the chestnut borer, the emerald ash borer (which had been moving through the region), and other destructive pests.

"There's a hundred different ways to kill a tree," Terry said, repeating a mantra familiar to loggers. "A chainsaw is only one." Terry was full of logging homilies, as a veteran logger should be, including this particularly practical piece of wisdom: "The safest place to be when a tree falls is right next to the stump—that way you know where it will land."

He also made the case that clear-cutting was bad news in Wisconsin's northern hardwoods, something rarely heard back in the days of the timber kings. Today, selection cutting is part of the business plan.

"An area that is clear-cut in our northern hardwoods takes more than fifty years to recover while leaving a void that is susceptible to erosion and soil depletion," Terry said. "You want to cut enough to let in sunlight so the understory can grow, but not too much."

After talking logs, Terry and his cousin Tim walked through the mill, following a ten-foot basswood log as it was sliced into 10 to 20-inch boards with a laser-guided saw in less than two minutes; they watched the bad lumber separate from good lumber on a high-speed conveyor belt, the bad to be made into chips, the good into blinds, but only after a complicated process of being edged, graded, planed, dried, cured, and stacked.

Terry climbed into his SUV and drove to the timberland he owned, pulling to a stop alongside a small bridge above a creek. He wanted to illustrate how water quality factored into the big picture of the woodlands. "This is a Class A trout stream. The trees need clean water, same as fish, from rainwater and from groundwater. If there's silt in this stream, it covers the trout eggs, and no trout. When we were kids we came out here and washed our cars. We didn't know any better."

He apparently knows better now. He built the bridge, he said, for several reasons. The practical reason was so logging trucks could have easier access. Before the bridge was built, logging trucks couldn't cross the creek when it flooded. The less obvious reason for the bridge was to provide improved water quality for the trout stream. When trucks had to drive through the creek, they compromised the creek bed and muddied the stream. Not anymore.

Terry's enthusiasm was nonstop.

So what got into Terry's head to make him such a tree hugger, as well as a tree logger?

He cited his grandfather with instilling everyone in the family with a sense of responsibility. "Grandpa Herman was such a utilitarian," Terry recalled. "He taught us to save some timber for the future. Don't cash in all your resources at one time because it's a long haul. If you take care of the forest, it'll take care of you." His father, Bud, "wasn't into conservation so much. Everybody's got a different point on the spectrum," Terry shrugged sympathetically. He had been the same way, once upon a time. "When I was younger, I was ready to cut down every tree, I didn't care what size it was, so I could turn it into dollars," he said. The urge to do right by nature "was intuitive, a self-educating thing" that evolved over the years.

His personal awakening came courtesy of a local timber manager named John Moran, who hired Terry, then a fresh-faced, eager-beaver, 22-year-old lumberjack, to help log a forest near Mellen. Moran instructed him to do selective harvesting. "He told us not to clear-cut, to be selective," remembered Terry. "Make it so you can come back in twenty years." The young logger followed instructions, but he didn't pay much attention to the reasoning behind it until John Moran hired Terry to return to the same forest in Upper Wisconsin twenty years later.

Then he saw the light. Terry couldn't tell where he had logged before. The area he'd once cut and the surrounding forest looked the same to eyes trained to pick out the best hardwoods. He fully understood what Moran was talking about.

Terry developed a timber management plan in the mid-1970s with Burns Forestry, a local timber management company that contracted with landowners to maximize their forest holdings. He also enrolled in state programs to learn about sustainable forestry.

Terry related this story while driving his Yukon on paved and unpaved roads winding through the woods until he found his brother, Gregg, in the middle of an unpaved road, sitting high in the cab of a slasher, a massive crane-sized piece of machinery that stacked cut logs, the operator separating them by length and species. Gregg was working what he described as an "above average" stand of hard maple, the kind with a small center heart and white wood that buyers look for. "I might get 20,000 board feet out of 200 cords of wood," he reckoned.

Some of the hardwoods the Peters were contracted to harvest for this current project had to be cut by hand, the old-fashioned way. It took a few minutes of wandering in the woods and stopping to listen before Terry located his cousin, Dale Guerin, wielding a chain saw and dressed

Trees logged by Terry Peters Logging (Photo by Jeff Peters)

in his safety pants, hard hat with eye and ear protection, steel-toe boots and a work-worn t-shirt advertising a book festival. Dale, who was in his mid 50s and had worked alongside Terry for twenty-two years, welcomed Terry when he spotted us coming his way. He took a break from thinning a stand of maple on a slope to talk about his job and the joys of working alone in the woods. He had cut between seventy and eighty trees that day—after sizing up each specimen and putting it into the context of the woods. After felling the timber, he used a skidder with a giant-size mechanical cable winch to grasp and drag the cut logs to the road where they would be hauled off.

This was Dale's second time to work this stand. "I was here in '92," he said. "We like to come back and see what we've done and the impact that we made." He had done such a good job the first time out, he had a hard time pinpointing the site again. Once he did, he liked what he saw and what he didn't see. His cuts had been made with surgical precision; there was no evidence of his previous cuttings, which tickled him to no end. "I have a lot of love for the woods because I have a lot of respect for them," Dale said.

Terry talked about how this particular stand of trees was growing atop a vein of iron ore that had been smoothed by glaciers advancing and retreating 15,000 years earlier. "It's all self-sustaining, it just has to be left alone," he said. "We have such a strong canopy. Last year, we had a drought and these hardwoods were the last green things left."

"Dale is unusual, he's a planner" Terry said, back behind the wheel of the Yukon after leaving his cousin to his solitude. "Some of the old European management philosophy is behind it. Logging selective hard-woods was a decision I made twenty years ago. I did it to get away from clear-cutting. Like Dale said, it gets boring. We saw the need to think fifteen to twenty years ahead. I remember the first time that forester [John Moran] told me, 'I want you to think about the forest in fifteen years.' The day we went back to that job, those trees were so beautiful. You can actually do this. It was good then, it's better now. It'll be better later. The circle is complete. We've got this endless cycle if we don't screw it up and there isn't some disease or a monster windstorm."

Peters slowed the vehicle when a noisy yellow machine flashed in the green mass of woods. Jamie Peters, Terry's 35-year-old son, was dozing a road through a county-owned forest with a Caterpillar. "Jamie's been in the woods seventeen years," Terry said as he flagged his son down. He'd trained to be a welder, decided it wasn't his calling, quit, and has been in the woods ever since.

The road Jamie was carving out of the forest would create access so the Peters family could retrieve 2,000 cords of timber that Terry had contracted to harvest, a task that would add almost $100,000 to the county coffers. "We're taking out a quarter of the trees," Terry said. "It will improve the health of the stand because we're taking out the worst of the worst." Ideally, there will be little visual evidence of the cutting.

A few miles away, another of Terry's sons, Corey, 31, was operating a processor, a $320,000 machine that he owned. The processor cuts trees on the spot, strips off branches and bark, and then stacks the logs. Corey got the logging bug when he was 12, peeling bark off pulpwood, like his brothers and his father before him. He became addicted when he started running equipment at 14. Corey figured the processor was a smart investment because it did the work in half the time it would take him by hand, saved him the effort of manual felling, and let him effortlessly "pick up sticks," as he put it.

Fifteen relatives in all worked for Terry, including Jamie and Corey, their brother Cody, Terry's brother, Gregg, his nephew Jake, and cousins Dale, Chris, and Randy. Working with family is easier than working with strangers because "we trust each other," Terry contended. Everyone works as independent contractors. Terry's wife, Kaye, and many of the wives of his sons, brothers, and cousins are teachers or work for city, county, state, and federal government agencies; their jobs provide health insurance, something loggers have difficulty purchasing on their own.

Despite a minimum of ten hours on the job each and every day, Terry likes to carve out enough time in his schedule to publicly advocate for sustainable forestry as the key to maintaining the way of life that the region was built upon. He is a featured speaker at the Northern Great Lakes Visitor Center, where he explains the Northwoods and its history to tourists. He sits on the advisory board of the Sigurd Olson Environmental Institute at Northland College in nearby Ashland, where he also lectures. He was a charter member of the Bad River Watershed Association and has been a lifelong supporter of the Great Lakes Timber Professionals Association, which champions sustainable timber products. He is also a proud participant in the Log A Load for Kids charitable timber harvest, a program that gets fourth and fifth grade elementary school children into the forest for an informative walk in the woods with Terry.

Sustainability and efficiency are buzzwords of every "stump" speech and casual conversation. Facts roll off Terry's tongue effortlessly, often without prompting: wood, unlike ethanol made from corn, returns eight times as much cellulose; usable forest grows at 4 percent a year; the mill under construction in Park Falls, about twenty-five miles south of Mellen, would be the first self-sustaining paper mill in the United States, with a biofuel refinery alongside it.

It makes perfect sense then, that Terry Peters got the call when The Nature Conservancy needed to prune a recent acquisition: the woods around the wetlands of Caroline Lake, which form the headwaters of the Bad River.

During summer months, Terry likes to end his days on the patio deck of his home, high on a ridge top above a vast sea of treetops. With a turn of his head, he can scan the horizon—Lake Superior and the Apostle Islands are visible in the far distance, and Chief Mountain in Michigan's Upper Peninsula is off to the right. The view provides perspective on his livelihood and his sense of place. So did the book in his lap on this particular day. It was his family's history. He pointed at old photographs, read descriptions carefully, and picked up a new detail about a cousin as he traced for me Thomas Larson's story all the way to his parents and their siblings.

He closed the book and surveyed the vista once again. "I've learned something new," he said with a satisfied smile as the woodlands disappeared in the fading light. "My day is complete."

Jim, Calvin, Teddi, Tim, Heather, and Frances Coleman (Photo by Bill Gillette)

CHAPTER 5

Coleman Ranches

Anyone can own a ranch, but it takes a rancher to care for the land. One of Jim Coleman's mottos is that if you take care of the land, the land will take care of you. It's this ethic that has grabbed attention in the conservation world and inspired many people to take innovative conservation approaches such as community-based conservation and working-lands conservation. Ranchers like Jim and Frances Coleman have embraced innovation to keep their ranches intact and help produce the world's food supply. They provide leadership—in their community and in their state—by voluntarily setting aside land for communal use. This allows them and their neighbors to move livestock between winter and summer ranges; it also assures that the land will still be there for their children's children and their children after them.

Visitors from around the world find that they love Colorado and want to live here. The state has a vibrant and economically significant agricultural industry. But Colorado is conflicted in its land use. Urban development and urban perceptions often plague the livelihood and lifestyle of Colorado ranchers. Looking at this conflict yields insight into the future of the state's ranching industry and its interplay with conservation. We're at a crossroads that offers both challenges and opportunities for the state's citizens to invest in conservation through ranching.

As Jim and Frances continue to expand their conservation ethic in an unassuming fashion throughout the San Luis Valley and neighboring valleys beyond, the legacy of their actions blazes new trails for conservationists and agriculturists alike. I can almost see the wry grin spreading across Jim's face as if he knew his plan would work all along and the rest of us are just now catching on.

—Terry R. Fankhauser,
Fifth Generation Rancher,
Executive Vice President,
Colorado Cattlemen's Association

AUTHOR'S NOTE: With great sadness I report that Frances Coleman passed away before the publication of this book. It is all the more fitting that her contributions to conservation are documented and celebrated here.

Tim Coleman at work on the ranch (Photo by Bill Gillette)

Jim and Frances Coleman enjoy showing visitors around their ranch, a legacy spread in the rolling foothills of southern Colorado's San Luis Valley. It's this ranch that birthed Coleman Natural Beef, the first natural beef program in the United States. Opening their land and their cattle operation has helped outsiders better understand the challenges the Colemans face every day, and they always find something new to learn from others.

They like to tell the story of the teenager touring the ranch with a group of Japanese students; the teen suddenly bolted from the pack and ran out into the middle of an alfalfa pasture, where he stripped off his clothes and shouted for joy at the top of his lungs.

The elderly couple understood the reaction.

"He'd never seen so much open country in his life," Jim chuckled.

The Colemans know that their spread in this exceptionally productive valley sandwiched between the soaring Sangre de Cristo Mountains to the east and the sprawling San Juan range to the west is special. Working to make it even better is a family tradition. Colemans have been seeking ways to improve their ranching and farming practices ever since James Coleman arrived from Altoona, Pennsylvania in 1872 to homestead in the valley. Jim, the patriarch of the current line of Colemans, has followed in those footsteps for more than fifty years, beginning when he returned to his hometown of Saguache after doing a tour in the military and earning his animal husbandry degree at Colorado State University; he arrived ready to put school-learned concepts to the test.

He became the first to erect crossfences on federal grazing lands in 1959 in order to prevent overgrazing, a practice that is now encouraged by government officials. "It was a hot and dry summer," Jim remembered, cracking a crinkled grin across his well-weathered face. "Didn't have much hay to put up and my dad was a good welder. We kept building fence until we got our ranges separated into pastures. Then we could rotate the cattle."

He was one of the first cattle ranchers in the San Luis Valley to embrace artificial insemination (AI) as a means to improve the herd. "We tried to get away from the big, big cow," he said about a trend that was once popular among cattle raisers. "Those big bulls eat too much. Some are so big, they don't grow. We wanted more efficient cattle." He experimented with Simmental and Limousin cattle in the 1960s before settling on Black Angus as the family's breed of preference.

The Coleman Ranch was the first property along Saguache Creek to have a conservation easement on their land, achieved with the help of the Colorado Cattlemen's Agricultural Land Trust. "Then another rancher clear up the creek decided to do it," Jim grinned proudly, fully aware of what he started. "Then everybody else decided to do it. Now almost all the ranchers are in conservation easements, meaning there won't be any development on this creek. This is the only creek in Colorado that's not developed."

The agreements formalized a cooperative system that had been in place for more than a century; they provide assurance that the ranching way of life along the creek will continue long after the current generation has passed.

Lately, Jim had been fiddling around with a solar panel project to provide running water for his cattle through the winter. "Water in winter time is the best feed," he said. "We're putting in solar as part of the Watershed Improvement Commission with the Natural Resources Conservation Service. There's an endangered species here, the southwest willow flycatcher, and they've got this program to save this little bird that nests in cottonwoods. The solar will cost $2,000 and NRCS is paying for half," he said.

Once the solar gets up and running, Jim's focus will shift to another "new deal," as he described it—using new ultrasound technology to determine if their Black Angus calves will fatten on grass, rather than the feed supplements given to most cattle before heading to the slaughterhouse.

Even Jim's ramshackle appearance speaks to his family's inventiveness. His weathered, rumpled cowboy hat, his dust-caked Levis 501s, scuffed boots, tattered team jacket, and the beat-up flatbed pickup truck he was steering were not for effect. "That's why I shop at Goodwill," Frances Coleman groused good-naturedly about the man she's been married to for more than fifty years, "Because he tears them all up. It doesn't matter if I buy him a $100 shirt. He's going to tear it up the first day he puts it on."

Jim and Frances's frugality is complemented by two other family traits—a love of hard work and an instinct for inventive improvisation, especially with found objects. That gene was reflected in Jim's playful blue eyes as he showed off some Coleman creations. The ranch shop was fashioned out of rail cars that had been previously used as a hog pen. The ceiling girders inside are discarded electric power poles. The boiler to heat the shop was made out of a steel pipe and a metal barrel; old fence posts, scrap wood, and used oil provide the fuel. Their cattle loader and feeders were fashioned by Jim and his son Tim from a railroad hopper car and lumber. Tim used metal fence posts to make cattle guards across fence lines that a motorcycle or four-wheeler could use. The snowplow they use to clear away snow for cattle and calves in the winter is a trailer hitch. "A path in the snow leaves a dry place for cattle to rest on," explained Tim. "They use less energy and eat less."

Nature has taken care of the rest. Despite the 7,700-foot elevation and a growing season under one hundred days, the Colemans' stock gets the most out of grazing forage so rich in nutrients that supplemental feed is rarely needed. The keys are the rich blue grama grasses in the three low-country pastures leased from the Bureau of Land Management and the abundant bunch grasses in the five high-country pastures in the Gunnison and Rio Grande national forests up on the continental divide that are leased from the U.S. Department of Agriculture.

In the early 1970s, Jim's brother Mel took note of the family's "clean" ranching ways, and set out to market Coleman Natural Beef. Mel knocked on numerous doors before he developed relationships with natural food stores across the United States, beginning with Mrs. Gooch's, a small Southern California chain.

"Natural is not too hard to do in this country," explained Jim. "Our cattle were always natural, really. We keep them healthy. We vaccinate calves at branding to prevent sickness, and if one gets sick, we go ahead and doctor him, save him if we can, but we wouldn't sell him on the open market because the calf didn't make it through the entire natural program process."

Their neighbors took note. "People started asking us what we were doing, but mainly, how they could get into the program," he related. "A lot of these ranchers around here, their cattle are all natural. All they have to do is if they doctor a calf, put a tag in his ear and sell him differently."

Mel Coleman and his family left the Saguache ranch for the big city to expand operations, eventually contracting with other ranches around the country. Coleman Natural Beef grew so large that the company was eventually sold to investors.

Leaving the ranch was never a consideration for Frances and Jim Coleman. They were rooted to the San Luis Valley. She spent more than fifty years working as a nurse in area hospitals and schools. He sat on grazing advisory boards and water district panels, and developed a reputation as an ardent water conservationist. The Coleman Ranch sits above an abundant aquifer, and the family has senior water rights. "I've always said, if you haven't got the water, you haven't got the grass, and if you haven't got the grass, you haven't got the cow, and if you haven't got the cow, you haven't got the cowboys," Jim reasoned.

The water, the grasses, and their careful management of both assets allows them to cut their hay two to three weeks earlier than most neighbors, which makes for better cattle feed. "The hay is more palatable to the cows if you cut it earlier," Frances said. "If you don't mow your lawn, it grows up, goes to seed, and dies. When you cut early, the grass is more nutritious and you don't have a weed problem. Besides, if you wait too long, the food value of the grass is lost."

With their son and daughter-in-law, Tim and Teddi, working and living on the ranch, along with their grandson Calvin, the future of the Coleman ranch is secure. But Jim and Frances, both in their seventies, are in no mood to slow down, preferring to work around the clock, their zeal for conservation and developing new strategies undiminished. There is always something to learn.

Jim began one mid-summer day by driving his pickup to check the five-mile pipeline that ran from a freshwater spring in the hills to water tanks on some wide flats on BLM lands seven miles east of the ranch house. Jim and Tim and Calvin built the pipeline to provide water for wildlife and habitat as well as their cattle. Tim and Teddi were spending the morning up in the high country, fifty miles west, herding cattle around their summer pastures in the Rio Grande National Forest. Frances was holding down the fort, paying bills, and feeding Calvin in the ranch house whenever the 16-year-old on a serious growth spurt stopped by the house between fixing fence line, baling hay, and other chores.

Calvin was raised by his parents and grandparents to ranch. He learned how to ride a horse about the same time he learned to walk and was operating farm equipment by age eight. During the school year, Calvin wakes up early to do chores with his grandfather from 5 A.M. to 7 A.M. every morning before going to high school, where he plays eight-man football (his grandmother is the team trainer). Calvin's older sister Heather also works on the ranch when she isn't attending college or working for the U.S. Forest Service in the summer. The kids are chips off the old block. So was Tim's sister, Cindy, who followed in her mother's footsteps and works as a nurse in Pueblo, Colorado, although she too returns to lend a hand around the ranch throughout the year.

Jim inspected each water tank (he was satisfied once he heard water trickling inside the tank), visited with a neighbor who lived near the pasture to discuss how his cows were behaving, then headed back to the house, where the master of the water district drove up to inspect Jim's charts. "He makes sure you're not cheating on your water," Jim said with a friendly nod as the water master scanned the numbers. "He'll shut you down if you've been taking too much from the ditch." As the Number 7 senior water rights holders in the valley, practically the whole San Luis Valley would have to go dry before the Colemans would be forced to cut back on their allotment of water for irrigation.

After lunch, Jim accompanied a field representative from the local office of the Natural Resources Conservation Service to inspect ten head gates he had constructed along the main irrigation ditch from Saguache Creek, which allow him to more efficiently water fields of alfalfa and clover. The head gates are opened every May, and each field is flooded with water for a day, per the Colemans' water rights. Before the new head gates were installed, the Colemans used tarps to direct the water flow, despite considerable waste. "Now, we get more water when we want it," Jim said with a smile of satisfaction. The NRCS was sharing the cost of construction and wanted to be certain the Colemans had adhered to

Calvin, Jim, and Tim Coleman (Photo by Bill Gillette)

NRCS standards. The field rep recorded each head gate with a Global Positioning System (GPS) to pinpoint its location. There was some good-natured back and forth about whether the head gate "wings" on some of the openings were wide enough to qualify for NRCS funding; if they weren't, a season's worth of work would be for naught. But the gates were ultimately approved.

There was a laundry list of to-do chores for the coming weeks while the weather was still pleasant: buying water tanks for a new project, laying pipe, and installing the new system would take them into the next week. After that, there was alfalfa to cut, with a third cutting scheduled for September before the first freeze. Although the days were still warm, five elk had already been sighted in the valley, a sure sign the cooldown was coming early this year. By late September, the whole family would be moving cattle from summer pasture in the high country down to the ranch and transporting the calves by truck.

With more than one hundred miles of fence to ride, there was always work to be done. Jim and Frances give the impression that if they didn't work, they wouldn't know what to do with themselves. As it was, Frances found plenty of reasons to complain about all the physical labor she couldn't do anymore at her age. She clearly does not like asking for help.

The reward for their toil is getting to share their story with others. "Colorado College sends out a class every year to see how we raise cattle and protect the land," Frances said. They are happy to do show and tell with anyone who asks, Frances explained, because people living in an increasingly urbanized world need to understand the ranching way of life and how it benefits city folks' lives.

"I see the snakes and lizards and horny toads go across the road. I see the rabbits, the deer, elk, antelope, and eagle," she said. "Some people don't see any of that stuff. They think there's nothing out there and they don't even look. So we take hikes to show the city kids what's out there. I take my grandkids on nature hikes, show them how to pick up snakes, learn the different kinds of tracks. But most people nowadays have no idea about any of this stuff."

Frances takes the same approach with the Coleman cattle. "We work our cows slowly and calmly. I talk to them and they understand. I can move a cow through a herd and into the barn by myself. I'll get out of my car and talk to them, 'OK girls, time to take a rest. Lay down.' They're my babies."

The family enjoys good relations with the federal agencies from whom they lease their grazing land, despite the inevitable turnover of government personnel. Tim Coleman keeps a diary record of range conditions in the high country that Teddi embellishes with botanical drawings of plants and grasses that they share with the feds. Frances engages them in her own way. "I tell the Forest Service we're damn sure not going to hurt the forest because we hurt ourselves if we do. It's hard to talk to some of them," she admitted. "They came from the cities, lot of 'em, and have the mentality that farmers and ranchers are screwing up the forest. It's hard to break them."

The family drives their summer herd into the high country of the Gunnison National Forest on horseback for fifty miles over four days around the first of June every year. Up top, the cattle graze in a cross-fenced pasture for twenty-one days before moving to one of two other pastures. Tim and Teddi commute between a cabin in the high country and their home near Jim and Frances's place until the herd comes down from the mountains in late September. "The range looks good up there," Tim reported one afternoon when the couple returned to the ranch. "We've got a lot of rain and it's greened up a bunch."

A soft-spoken cowman with a distinctive Fu Manchu mustache and a kerchief almost always tied around his neck, Tim Coleman was known around the valley for his AI skills, which he learned from his father and his grandfather, and was the focus of his college studies. "Tim's really good at getting those cows pregnant," his wife said teasingly. He allowed that he'd artificially inseminated 600 cows in one breeding season. He is happy to help out other ranchers who hire him for his expertise whenever he can spare the time.

But his job, as he sees it, is to continue what his parents and grandparents have done so that his own son and daughter can take up where he leaves off. "We're always trying to improve the herd, with different breeding, better facilities to work with, growth, milking ability, better marbling," he said. "AI is cost effective. The whole program has gotten better, the conception rate's better."

The constant quest to improve is a cornerstone of the Coleman family values, a trait Jim thinks came from his father "because he was always doing things conservative. He could make things out of nothing. He liked to develop the grass. Instead of getting bigger, he wanted to get better." Wherever it came from, everyone agrees that being in such a bountiful part of God's country influences everything they do, why they are there, why they ranch, and why they feel so alive.

"Some people see the land in terms of dollars and wealth," Teddi Coleman said. "We think you can't put a price on that water, that field. We live in what I call rustic elegance. We don't have frills, but we have all this natural elegance around us."

That natural elegance is the Colemans' whole reason for being.

Bradford, Aaron, Philip, Kendra, Marissa (seated), Susan, Charlene, Randall, and Joseph Lange

(Courtesy LangeTwins Winery and Vineyards)

LangeTwins Winery and Vineyards

As committed ambassadors of environmentally responsible, economically savvy and socially equitable land management practices, the Lange family of LangeTwins Winery and Vineyards in Lodi, California has power in numbers.

To ensure a thriving business and environment for years to come, the Twins (brothers Randy and Brad, along with their spouses, Char and Susan) have successfully, as Virginia farmer Joel Salatin puts it, "romanced the next generation." The fifth generation of cousins has returned to Lodi to help shape the family business. They return to land originally brought under Lange care by their great-great-grandparents—and none of them would rather be anywhere else.

Applying lessons learned from running a multi-generational family farm, the Langes are influencing a cleaner, greener direction for the wine industry. Community leadership, information sharing, and a pioneering spirit are all key to this process. From wildlife habitat and water conservation, to renewable energy production and integrated pest management, the Langes lead by example and readily share the successes and challenges of their ongoing efforts to redefine "business as usual" in the Golden State and beyond.

As the executive director of a non-profit organization that partners with the private sector to identify and implement environmental solutions that make economic sense, I greatly respect the Langes' "can-do" approach to land stewardship and business problem solving. By growing partnerships—at the dinner table, on the farm, and in the board room—the Langes bolster not only their own, but also their neighbors' and fellow industry members' ability to address natural resource constraints, engage in restoration projects, and turn a profit.

Win-win-wins for wildlife, human health, and agriculture—power in numbers indeed.

—Ashley Boren,
Executive Director, Sustainable Conservation

Vineyard (Courtesy LangeTwins Winery and Vineyards)

"This is peak period, this is payday," Brad Lange half-shouted as he swiveled around in his office chair, appearing lean, intense, and animated all at once. Although the morning sun had barely broken over the horizon, he had already made a run out to the fields to check on the grape harvest before returning to the office to determine exactly where his trucks, mechanical harvesters, and workers needed to be, analyzed a computer spreadsheet to determine irrigation schedules, and fixed a broken water pump. As his walkie-talkie squawked with the voices of five supervisors coordinating machines and work crews, Brad simultaneously engaged in discussions with his nephew, Aaron, who was reaching the end of his twelve-hour shift overseeing the harvest, and with his co-manager Kelly Brakel.

His urgency spoke to the task at hand: managing twenty vineyards comprising 7,000 acres spread across fifty miles, multitasking and juggling all the way. "You're witnessing a family that works together and plays together," he enthused, as he clicked on the walkie-talkie to bark a response before resuming the conversation. "Our family is not in this business by accident."

Harvest time was crunch time around the LangeTwins vineyards, as it has been ever since Brad and Randy Langes' grandfather, Albert, switched from dry-land farming melons to grapes in 1916. The twins, 58, are the great-grandchildren of Johann and Maria Lange, who left Germany in the 1870s to seek a better life in Lodi, where they started off farming melons on a small patch of land.

Every Lange since then has known that all hands are on deck and on call from the middle of August to October every year when the harvest comes in. Modern times are no different, but now the round-the-clock harvest is more intense: giant, noisy, twenty-foot-tall mechanized harvesters shake the trellised vines and pick the grapes in the very early morning, when the temperatures are coolest. After the grapes are separated from the vine comes the critical morning hours of loading six tons of grapes into bins on flatbed trailers waiting in the field, then hitching the trailers to semi trucks to haul the load to the winery, where the grapes are dumped onto a conveyor belt, separated, and then crushed before going into fermentation tanks and aging casks—and eventually becoming fine wine. Brad's role in this complicated process at this particular moment was making sure harvesters weren't idling because they had nowhere to dump their grapes.

Over the course of eight weeks, anywhere from 40,000 to 55,000 tons of chardonnay, sauvignon blanc, pinot grigio, pinot noir, merlot, zinfandel, cabernet sauvignon, petit verdot, syrah, and seven other varietals grown by LangeTwins would be picked, processed, crushed, fermented, and aged: each ton of grapes would yield 170 to 180 gallons of wine.

"We're not diverse in terms of crops," Brad said offhandedly. It's wine or nothing. They wouldn't have it any other way.

Brad slapped the sides of bins on the truck trailer to make sure they were empty before a John Deere tractor unloaded a load of grapes. "Double dump, put grapes in a bin that's already full of grapes, you've lost a lot of time and money," he said as he flipped through a stack of papers in his pickup and listened as static-frizzed voices on the walkie-talkie bounced from English to Spanish. "The guy who screws that up, is in the tank, so to speak," he winked. It was such a potential nightmare, he said, turning somber, that more than once he had awakened in the middle of the night to drive to bins in the field to slap their sides, to make doubly sure they were empty.

During the growing season, Brad splits irrigation duties with Kelly Brakel, who has worked for the Lange family since he and Brad and Randy were teenagers. That job entails inspecting the fields on an ATV. "I have to take a look at the vineyard, see what the vine is telling me in terms of water need, what the weather report says, what the computer analysis is telling us, and mix it up with my experience and Kelly's experience, and make decisions," Brad said. Boots on the ground are required to ensure coyotes haven't chewed up the drip irrigation hoses or a valve hasn't been stolen, and to take petioles—young leaf stalks—to the lab where they can be dried and crushed for nutritional analysis, so fertilizer can be applied frugally.

With an average sixteen inches of rain annually, the Langes rely heavily on forty-five deep wells that pump groundwater from an underground aquifer for irrigation. "If it weren't for the Sierra Nevada to the east of us, this valley would be a desert," Brad said. "Even so, the water table below is dropping precipitously."

Randy, the other Lange twin brother (the one with the gray crew cut who is not quite so intense), was down the road at the winery, weighing a load of merlot that had been delivered by grower Gary Patterson. The $20 million winery was built four years ago to handle 40,000 tons of grapes a day as a means to "add value to our product," as Randy described it politely. More to the point, the winery was the key to keeping the business in the family. The winery vertically integrates the Langes' grape-farming operation into a soil-to-glass system that allows them to either process their own grapes (rather than selling them to other wineries) or to process other growers' grapes, including loads destined for well-known Napa area wineries. The winery's design includes concrete pads with future expansion in mind.

"When the kids made the decision to come back to the farm, we, as a family, started to take a look at the changing dynamics of the business," Randy explained as he showed off the state-of-the-art facility. "Brad and I and our father spent our careers as contract growers, but I don't think the next generation will be able to do just that. So we made decisions four years ago to try and ensure the fifth generation and the sixth generation will have the opportunity to farm. We have to make wine. We have to put our name on the bottle. We have to go out and sell our product and put a personality behind the product. It was the only way they could have a legitimate opportunity to stay in the family business."

Brad and Randy will be a tough act to follow. They've grown their business artfully as they increased their acreage, beginning with 126 acres purchased from their parents in 1980. The California wine industry was then on the cusp of becoming a major global player, transitioning from an era when grapes were still picked by hand.

To make ends meet, Brad and Randy formed a management company, growing grapes for winemakers such as Gallo, and their friend Bob Mondavi, who would eventually earn recognition as the father of the modern California wine industry. Charlene Lange, Randy's wife, earned a salary by working on converting the old Lodi High School into a civic center, and Susan Lange, Brad's wife, brought in a steady paycheck as a speech language therapist for Lodi public schools. With Brad and Randy driving trucks and manning harvesters, the brothers were able to plow whatever profits they made from the management contracts into buying more land, by then totaling more than 1,400 acres, while continuing to look for ways to economize and innovate. By the time the new winery became a reality, Susan was running the LangeTwins business office while Char handled marketing and public relations.

Brad and Randy were the first in Lodi to use the bilateral cordon trellis system and the vertical shoot position trellis that guides the growth of vines to allow mechanical harvesters to more efficiently move down the crop rows and collect grapes. It was Randy who suggested add-ons to the first Gregoire harvesters they purchased, including an air filter for the driver cab that is now a standard feature on the $250,000 machine.

"We were doing sustainable work twenty years ago," Randy said. "It was out of respect for the land. Honestly." They took it upon themselves to restore riparian corridors as they learned more over the years about the role these corridors played in the health of river habitat. "These sloughs that go through here, where my grandfather took out trees to put in vineyards, we've taken out the vineyards, removed cattle from the sloughs, and planted trees again. Now we have oak trees out there that are eight inches in diameter, ten feet tall. We're allowing the natural grasses to come back in. You either believe in it or you don't."

Randy left no question where his family stood.

"We never sat down and said, 'We've got to change the way we do things.' We saw so many things in the same way it wasn't a conscious decision. We just did it. Our chillers run on glycol, which is more environmentally responsible. We have solar panels on roofs [which provide 80 percent of the power needs of the water pumps, their homes, office and shop]. Every gallon of water we use ends up used for irrigation or put on the pasture. We changed the [water] demand for our crops," he said, citing the Langes' embrace of drip irrigation to reduce water consumption. The family had calculated they would use seven gallons of water for every gallon of wine produced. "But we actually use only about two gallons of water for every gallon of wine," Randy said.

The settling ponds that process wastewater outside the winery effectively function as wetlands. "There's a levee under those aerators," he said, pointing toward the ponds out back. "The ponds biodigest solids and sugars. All the solids go to the bottom, where they're digested. The

Solar panels in the Lange family vineyards (Courtesy LangeTwins Winery and Vineyards)

clean water goes over the top of the levee. You're not going to smell that pond because we're running it right. It's got the correct pH."

"We spent a lifetime examining the way we farm," Randy said as he walked from the ponds to a rheumatic 18-wheeler loaded with a trailer load of pomace—the grape skins and stems that are removed at the winery. He was going to drive the load to a field where the pumice would be dumped and spread as fertilizer. "We want to farm better and have less

of an impact on the environment we're farming in and less of an impact on our families. We've improved our equipment. We use insecticides and fungicides only when we have to, and developed a sprayer with four arms, instead of one, to reduce the carbon footprint. We walk our vineyards to assess what's happening, and we pull the trigger on a crop protection product only when necessary."

Perhaps the Langes' biggest leap of faith was in signing California's first Safe Harbor Agreement (SHA) for private property owners. In exchange for restoring habitat for endangered species, these agreements protect landowners from prosecution for accidentally killing an endangered species. Brad got interested in SHAs when the valley elderberry longhorn beetle was listed as threatened by U.S. Fish & Wildlife in 1980. The beetle lived in elderberry bushes found in riparian areas, 90 percent of which had been destroyed for agricultural use in the Lodi/Sacramento Delta area. Brad engaged environmentalists, developers, and state and federal authorities to find common ground, and he formed a committee that included growers in the Sacramento Delta.

"I started looking at our river, particularly the lower reaches of the Mokelumne, which runs through our land," he explained. "I got this group together with the local resource conservation district and formed a committee to write a stewardship plan and work paper." Along the way, he learned about Safe Harbor, a concept developed by U.S. Fish & Wildlife and the Environmental Defense Fund to encourage landowners to restore and maintain critical habitat. Working with Fish & Wildlife personnel and Michael Bean from the Environmental Defense Fund, Brad helped write a recovery plan for the beetle; in 2006, he became the first landowner to sign on to a Safe Harbor Agreement. His charge was to plant elderberry bushes and restore riparian areas around rivers, sloughs, and wetlands on his land to protect the endangered beetle; to attract wildlife, he would build boxes for wood duck and owls. So far, the Langes have restored Gill Creek and rehabilitated a quarter-section of slough. Last year, they counted seventy wood duck hatchlings and observed that most of the seventy-four strategically placed owl boxes were occupied.

Brad also became a founding board member of the Lodi-Woodbridge Winegrape Commission and served as its first chairman, a position now held by his daughter, Kendra. The coalition of the growers in Lodi organized in 1991 to better market the region, which lacks the curb appeal of adjoining Napa and nearby Sonoma counties. A key strategy in raising the profile of the Lodi appellation was a sustainable viticulture certification program called Lodi Rules. The program's standards include economic and social equity and environmental viability. Seventeen Lodi wineries, including LangeTwins, have been certified to carry the Lodi Rules sustainable wine certification, the first such sustainable wine program in the state.

All the adjustments are about the future.

In a low-slung building tucked behind the winery, three of the five cousins representing the next generation of Langes were brainstorming how to build the LangeTwin brand. A sustainable winegrowing marketing campaign and a Web-based wine club are already in place. Specific areas of California and elsewhere were being targeted, along with regional distributors. The Lodi Rules sustainable wine certification program has been launched. It was time to get rolling.

The eldest of the five Lange cousins, Marissa, 31, Randy's daughter, was fully aware of the high stakes. "Our four parents bet the farm to see this happen," she said, explaining why she never used her degree in neuroscience and instead did sales and marketing for Robert Mondavi and marketing and brand management for Foster's Wine Estates in Napa before returning to the family business in 2005 to develop the LangeTwins's business plan. "I wasn't going back to the family farm. That was not where my core competencies were," she said. But when the family farm grew into another kind of business, she heeded the call. "The gravitational pull back is pretty strong. But we didn't just want to [come back]. We were needed."

Brad's daughter Kendra, 26, followed in her cousins' footsteps, interning and then working at Foster's Wine Estates before joining the family to do brand marketing, wholesale, and direct sales. "Once we started talking about the winery," she said. "I knew I was coming back. I knew I would come back sooner or later, because I like being in Lodi. This is only our second vintage, so we have time to figure out who we are and who we want to be. We know we're family. We know we're sustainable. We have to find the right channel and go."

Marissa's younger brother Joe, 25, a crew-cut, casual kid partial to flip-flops, was wine-focused from the get-go, graduating from Cal Poly with degrees in agriculture business, and wine and viticulture; he also studied practical viticulture and wine sciences at the University of Adelaide, Australia. Now he oversees the LangeTwins's Web site, blog, wine club, and direct sales—when he isn't managing the day-shift harvest and maintenance crews.

"I love working in the fields, but I also love to dork it out on computer and interacting with customers," he said. When harvest rolls around, he manages to combine both pursuits by blogging about bringing in the grapes.

Aaron, Randy's 28-year-old son, complements Joe's academic track and work interests, having studied viticulture at UC Davis and spending six months working at a winery in Chile before coming back to Lodi. He now works on IT and human resources matters; his fluency in Spanish comes in handy when working with field crews.

Brad's son, Philip, is practically Aaron's twin brother—they were born just eleven days apart. Philip studied agricultural mechanics and viticulture at Fresno State and UC Davis. Now he's in charge of LangeTwins's vineyard operations, the labor force, pesticide management and equipment maintenance.

The winery puts all this combined knowledge and experience to work. Will their strength in numbers allow them to grow a wine and a winery in a hyper-competitive market?

"The idea of making our own wine was always fermenting," Marissa said (pun wholly intended). "Our winemaker, David Akiyoshi learned his craft from Bob Mondavi, but when Mondavi was bought out, David left and suggested making wine together. We took his idea of making a couple hundred cases, and made it a much bigger vision. It went from a casual conversation to a finished building in about eighteen months."

The cousins' participation means that there are nine Type-A personalities in the family mix, a potentially volatile combination. "We all have our opinions," Marissa conceded. "But we all grew up together on the compound, if you will, where it was two families living together. We know how to vacation together. [The family takes annual treks together, as far-ranging as Patagonia, Peru, Kilimanjaro, Sikkim, and Nepal.] We know how to work together, to agree to disagree and to listen to other opinions and achieve consensus—which isn't necessarily pleasing everyone."

At nine o'clock one evening in the middle of harvest, Philip and Aaron Lange said their goodbyes around the dinner table at Char and Randy's before heading off to work, with Aaron fidgeting visibly. "If you think we're a family of neurotics, he takes the cake," Brad grinned, nodding toward Aaron, never mind that Brad had been working seventeen hours straight.

Aaron was still in the field the next morning as the sun cast early morning shadows over the vineyards, yakking in Spanish into the walkie-talkie. He was still fidgeting as he paused to count the reasons why he thought he had the best job in the whole world. "I was not the ranch FFA-type kid. I was a super nerd—number two in my class. My first college major was managerial economics. I still handle all the IT and human relations stuff for our company. When I get done here, I'll go home, check on my e-mail, to see if there are any problems. Carrying on the family business, working for yourself, growing something, communicating with people, dealing with different cultures, there are so many intangibles, and you work your ass off. I get that desk time, and at night in the fields, I get to look up at Cassiopeia and Orion."

The placid expression on his face, illuminated by the morning sunlight, said all the rest, leaving no question where the LangeTwins brand was headed.

Michelle, Sidney, Hadley, Barbara, and Norman Pape (front); Fred, Logan, and David Pape (back) (Photo by Crystal Lawrence)

CHAPTER 7

Pape Ranches

You are about to read the story of the ranching accomplishments of the Pape family of Daniel, Wyoming. Along with improving their agricultural operation and conserving their land resource, they have placed great emphasis on wildlife protection, which includes providing safe passage for the nation's largest seasonal movement of pronghorn antelope. I am so very impressed.

As outstanding as their record is, I have not yet mentioned what amazes me the most about them. They stand out from the pack above all, because of the inner strength of their family.

The Papes' daily discussions around their kitchen table are filled with lessons for us all. Most of us have families. As wonderful as families are, getting along is full of challenges. I am sure they have—and have had—many of the same problems that all of us face. Through the generations, however, they have managed to overcome the normal obstacles.

I can't possibly list all of the positives here. Their oneness of purpose, the value of each individual's contribution, the priorities of conservatism, family values, service to the community, overcoming adversity. . . . I could go on. You also get the feeling that they instinctively know that what they are doing is right.

It is not easy being somebody's hero. It is not something that you intensely prepare for, execute, and then relax and forget. It is a job every day for a lifetime. We all want to pass something valuable down to our children. In this case, through each generation, what was passed was a wonderful example.

  —Jon Kirkbride, Fourth Generation Rancher,
  President 2007–2009,
  Wyoming Stock Growers Association

The Pape Ranches (Photo by Crystal Lawrence)

The view from the highway was pastoral—pronghorn antelope, the fastest land animal in North America, and mule deer, icon of the American West, lounged in luxuriant grasses while black and red cattle browsed in a pasture nearby. Both the wildlife and the livestock looked very much at home on this majestic plain in northwest

Wyoming. The plain itself is enveloped by the Wind River Mountains to the east, the Gros Ventre Mountains to the north, and the Wyoming range to the west, with the Green River winding along the base of its verdant foothills.

The hand-carved wooden sign by the main gate from the highway reads "Welcome to Cattle Country," but there is so much wildlife in every direction, the sign could just as well declare "Drive-by Zoo." Canada geese floated on the small pond above a small stream where brook trout and rainbow trout thrived. Sage-grouse rambled inside fenced hay stacks and in the grasses beyond, within eyeshot of Sandhill cranes picking their way through wetlands and red tail hawks circling overhead.

Wild coexisting with domestic has always been a way of life on the Pape Ranches. Frederick Herman Pape first came into the area in the late 1800s with his three brothers and purchased the first 160 acres of Home Place, the name the ranch still retains. In 1917, Frederick's son, Lester, decided to try and make a living out of running a herd of one hundred Columbia ewes. Lester used to tell his son, Norm, that if he couldn't deal with moose raiding their haystacks, he ought to go back to Kansas where the Papes came from. Norm never gave it a thought. "This is almost like the Serengeti," he marveled, looking out the kitchen window of the house he has lived in all his 78 years. And he wasn't kidding. The Pape Ranches of northwest Wyoming are located in the southern part of the Greater Yellowstone Ecosystem, the last remaining large, nearly intact mountain ecosystem in the United States; it retains the greatest number of living organisms that have existed since pre-Columbian times. Pronghorn antelope pass through the ranches on their annual 180-mile migration, one of the longest land mammal migrations on earth.

Norm Pape is the current head of the Pape Ranches. And he taught his own boys what his father taught him. His son, Dave, (Frederick's great-grandson) told me, "The wildlife was here first. We manage around the wildlife," he said before correcting himself. "We manage *with* the wildlife. I was always raised that wildlife had a place and we better respect that because that's the way it is."

Quaking aspen and cottonwood leaves fluttered outside while Dave, 44, and his brother Fred, 46, sat around the breakfast table mapping out their day with their father and their mother, Barb, a steely, attractive blue-eyed woman with snow white, perfectly coiffed hair. Dave was headed six miles north to the McDole Place, a separate Pape Ranches property, with a tractor and mower (a "sagebrush beater") to an area where cattle were having trouble getting through. Fred was going along with him to cut firewood out of a stand of beetle-infested lodgepole pine on the Rosene Place, another of the Pape Ranches farther north. Barb was juggling bills that needed paying and had fall events to plan. Norm was on the phone helping organize the upcoming meeting of the Hoback Stock Association, seven ranchers who hold summer grazing leases in the Bridger-Teton National Forest. Once he finished that, he needed to drive his pickup across the highway to inspect a head gate that Dave had built. The head gate was designed to back-up creek water and create a wetland and winter watering area for their cows and for wildlife.

Mother, father, and sons had a precise schedule to keep. Winter was coming. Three days earlier, on the last day of August, the ranch had already received a dusting of snow and a hard freeze, cutting short the normal 64-day growing season in this high country, 7,300 feet above sea level.

The Papes' lives revolve around tending to 2,700 head of "Black Baldies," Red Hereford-Black Angus crossbred cattle, 10,000 acres of open range and irrigated farmlands, and grazing leases on over 100,000 acres of federal, state and private lands. They breed their stock with more than fifty bulls. They hire no extra help. They take pride that no one in the family has had to take a town job to keep the ranch going.

It had been only a decent year so far. "It wasn't a good spring," Norm said, referring to a dearth of moisture, "but I'm pleased sage-grouse numbers are good." The wild bird count is an indicator of the overall health of the habitat.

The herd calved in April through the end of May, before most of the cattle were moved into leased grazing lands in the high country for summer. By August, three generations of Papes gathered to make hay from the fields, the single cutting yielding exceptionally protein-rich hay. They purchased their feed conservatively, only after calculating the carrying load of each pasture.

By the end of October, the hay would be put up, all fences fixed, and cattle shipped off to market. "The cattle either gained well, or they didn't," Norm said of his favorite time of the year. At that point, all he'd be able to do is enjoy the brief respite. "You can catch your breath. You can go hunting, visit your buddies, take the time to do what you want to do. There are no insects, the nights are cool, days are nice, you can look back and see what you've accomplished."

Whenever questions are raised around the breakfast table during planning sessions, someone in the family sooner or later instinctively reaches for one of the annual diaries stuffed into a bookcase. The diaries contain observations about temperature, rainfall, and range conditions—the written records of ranch life since 1927, the year Lester and Mary married. "This is monitoring, this is what keeps us on track," Norm beamed, holding up a bound notebook marked 2007. "We can go back years to see what happened on that day. We go to the book."

Father, mother, and sons divvied up chores effortlessly. "We've worked together so long," Dave said, "that we don't have to really discuss a whole lot." Fred concurred. "We all work on machinery, we all fence and we all work on irrigation." Getting something done is not an issue. Each has their specialty. Fred built the addition to his house and the beds for his kids. Dave did horn art and liked to push boulders into creeks running through the Home Place to create trout habitat.

The whole Pape family history has been defined by improving the land for the benefit of their stock and the wildlife that lived among them. The roadside view told the story. Ninety years ago, when the working cattle ranch was established, if there had been such things as automobiles and state highways, a motorist would have looked at a decidedly different landscape—a vast sea of sagebrush and little more.

The wetlands, the lush irrigated pastures, and all the other features that attract wildlife are the direct result of years of hard work, careful planning, and exceptional vision by Norm and Barb, Dave and Fred, Fred's wife, Michelle, and Dave's wife, Naomi, who had recently passed away. Before them came Lester and Mary, and Lester's parents, Frederick Herman and Lena. Fred and Dave have an older sister, Jane Ann Potempa, who lives and works in southern California with her husband, Chuck, but she comes back for the family's annual branding and so does her daughter, Mary Barbara, 10, and her 8-year-old son, Joe, who has more than a little cowboy blood in him, according to his grandparents.

Land and cattle management require not only water, irrigation, brush and wildlife management, but also the fiscal discipline to retain enough liquidity to be able to afford to buy additional acreage if and when neighbors approached them to sell.

The longer he's ranched, the more Norm has made wildlife management his priority.

"Dad was a hunter and so was granddad," he said. "Most of the early people were. What wildlife was here was the source of food. Dad and Mother enjoyed watching people hunt and visiting with people." His personal appreciation of wildlife was enhanced by serving on the Wyoming Game and Fish Commission for six years beginning in 1987. His frequent absences to attend to commission business required Fred and Dave to make decisions on their own and grow into the job out of necessity.

A considerable amount of the Papes' time and effort is devoted to sagebrush. It has always been so. As soon as the first Papes and other homesteaders settled the Upper Green River more than a hundred years ago, they began grubbing out the coarse, hardy bush that dominates the drier parts of the Intermountain West region. At first, they did it to make gardens, then they did it to open up range and pastures for cattle. Sagebrush outcompetes grasses and other brush for what little rainfall falls, which is reason enough to keep it from spreading. Doing that requires the use of fire and water and lots of hard work. Fred and Dave followed in their father and grandfather's footsteps trying to bring back the native grasses that had been forced out by the sagebrush.

They have all been cautious about removing too much sagebrush, though. Wildlife such as the sage-grouse, a high prairie native in decline, depends on sagebrush for their survival. "That's one reason why we spray in a random mosaic pattern," Fred said of the family's prudent use of herbicides to contain sagebrush that they do in partnership with the Natural Resources Conservation Service. "We want to catch snow [with sagebrush] and leave enough for the deer, antelope, and the sage-grouse," Norm said, pointing out that all three species have significant populations on the Pape Ranches.

Something else that has proved effective in keeping sagebrush at bay is water. Sagebrush is a prodigious water-user in the usual dry conditions, but too much water does it in. "Water, over time, kills sagebrush, so over time, the homesteaders moved the water away from the river," Norm related. "We have four diversion points out of the Green River here at Pape Ranches. They moved that water, made these green areas, made these meadows, made these willows and wetlands, made all of this."

Better grazing land translated into better wildlife habitat; the new forbs drew increased numbers of resident and migrating species. Whatever could be seen from the roadside viewing area of the Pape Ranches was the result of a hundred years of Papes working the land hard, pushed along by deliberate thought and careful consideration.

The Papes welcome hunters and fishermen onto designated parts of their land at no charge, as long as their licenses are signed by Norm Pape or someone from the family. Pioneer hunters over seventy years of age and disabled hunters can take advantage of a special area set aside for them to enjoy the great outdoors and take a shot at a mule deer, antelope, and even elk that they would otherwise not have the opportunity to chase. Again, at no charge.

"There may not be financial benefit," Norm admitted. "But we benefit just to see that wildlife is here, that we provided habitat for it, that we're in a unique part of the world where there is wildlife movement back and forth like this. Golly sakes, nobody else has that opportunity."

Sandhill cranes on the Pape Ranches (Photo by Crystal Lawrence)

More than 150 friends, family, and neighbors come to the Papes' annual branding on the Mershon Place, which Norm's parents bought in 1946. "One way we can educate people is when they come to visit," he stated. "You show them how it works. We gave some staunch environmentalists in Pinedale a private tour and then invited them to a public tour. It's an opportunity to expand environmental and conservation awareness [about] how we provide habitat for wildlife and provide public joy through hunting, fishing, and just driving by the highway."

Frugal management has allowed them to extend the largesse. "The thing about this ranch was, there wasn't a lot of debt against this outfit, or a mortgage," Norm said. He and his father never overextended. They upgraded equipment when they could still get a resale price out of the machinery they were replacing. Whenever they purchased new property, they paid it off before they bought more.

The ranch was always first and foremost, and making sacrifices in order to get the operation through another season was often required. Norm, for instance, spent five years at the University of Wyoming, but he didn't get a degree. "There were a couple of springs [in college] I stayed home to help with the ranch work because we didn't have any help," he said. But he learned what he needed, and saw enough of the world during a two-year hitch with the Army (well, Fort Benning, Georgia, at least) to conclude he belonged on the ranch.

Fred and Dave received degrees in agribusiness from the University of Wyoming before they, too, returned—with new ideas about brush control, improving habitat for wildlife, and growing better grass. Range monitoring, cross fencing, pasture rotation, and livestock watering systems were implemented. Irrigated meadows now provide winter feed for both stock and wildlife. It's all part of long-range planning. "We determine what each of these pastures will carry over a period of seven years," Fred said, pointing out areas on an aerial map where they were resting pastures.

The wetlands created by their water management and storage innovations reflect the philosophy driving the operation of the ranches. "People say, why don't you drain those wetlands and create more meadow?" Norm admitted. "The boys just about come off their chairs when they hear that. They know we can utilize those wetlands late in the year if we need to." Twenty acres were dedicated to testing spring grazing forage. The Papes have also installed new, game-friendly fencing that keeps cattle in but allows antelope and deer to roam freely. They've also fenced around willow stands to provide windbreaks and keep livestock out of riparian areas.

But even as they modernize and adapt, new obstacles loom in the distance. The scattering of homes popping up to the north around Forty Rod Flat is growing every year, and that worries Norm. Smaller plots of land mean land fragmentation, which presents huge negatives as far as livestock and wildlife are concerned. More housing could disrupt how Pape Ranches do their business—and how the pronghorn antelope migrate.

Ranchers more set in their ways might think that another potentially disruptive problem is that the next generation of Papes living on the ranch is all women. Fred's wife, Michelle, 15-year-old Hadley, Dave's daughter, and her cousins Sydney, 16, and Logan, 18, Fred's daughters, have all embraced the ranching lifestyle; they act as the ranch's hay crew and are active in 4-H at their high school in Pinedale. Once they've gone off to college, perhaps they'll bring back husbands who will want to ranch too, Norm and Barb mused.

"It's a good question that we ponder from time to time," Norm said. "We may not come out and say, 'What's going to happen down the road? Who's going to take over for the sixth generation with a good outfit?' But this is a family operation. Most of the good ranches are still in existence and have family to take care of business, and they're not depending on a lot of labor because it's not available. Who knows? Barb and I aren't going to live forever. We're just here for a short time."

He knows the ranch will endure, as it should; the fruits of his and Barb's labor will remain for all to see. That roadside view of Pape Ranches from the highway will be just as majestic one hundred years from now. He also knows they have raised their sons and their sons raised their daughters well enough to know the best has yet to come for Pape Ranches. Fred remarked, "We're just stewards on this land, just like my great-grandfather and my dad. They've all made positive moves to make this land better."

Brian Treadwell (Photo by Chase Fountain)

CHAPTER 8

Treadwell Brady Ranch

Pioneer stockmen in the hill country region of Central Texas undoubtedly found conditions to their liking. Early reports from those ranching families described a landscape replete with unbroken native grasslands "stirrup high," spring-fed creeks and rivers, and woods and waters rich with fish and game. By all accounts, it was a region well suited to raising a family and making a living—largely through the production of sheep, goats, and cattle.

Much has changed since then. Today, there aren't many heritage ranching families left; where they can be found, they are confronted with challenges their forefathers never anticipated. Those expansive grasslands have been invaded by thick stands of Ashe juniper. Once-prolific springs have been diminished or have gone dry. Favorable incentives for the production of wool and mohair have been substantially reduced. Fragmentation of large parcels is now the norm, and land prices have escalated to the point where it is difficult to pass land from one generation to the next.

Suffice to say, it takes a special kind of ranching family to make ends meet in today's ranching climate. The Treadwells, whose family has been ranching in the Ft. McKavett area since the 1800s, epitomize that kind of family. Through innovation, experimentation, and an uncommon dedication to restoring, enhancing, and creatively using their ranch's bountiful natural resources, the father-son team of John and Brian Treadwell has made it work.

As owners and managers, the Treadwells exemplify the best in Texas' private lands stewardship. It is because of their rigorous commitment to prescribed fire and other habitat management tools, their innovative management of white-tailed deer and other wildlife, their well-planned grazing management program, and their systematic approach to caring for their lands and waters, that the Treadwells have received the state's prestigious Leopold Conservation Award, Texas' highest stewardship honor.

—Carter Smith, Executive Director,
Texas Parks and Wildlife

Treadwell Brady Ranch (Photo by Chase Fountain)

Treadwell had been working the arid grasslands around Fort McKavett in the Big Country of west Central Texas since 1888, shortly after the fort was erected to fend off hostile Comanche and Kiowa. Buffalo still roamed the open range and the howl of the red wolf could be heard when W. W. Treadwell established his thirty-six section ranch six miles north of the fort; he purchased the land from the state of Texas for a pittance down and the promise to pay the balance.

The first three generations of Treadwells made quite an impact on the arid lands. Cattle were purchased and put on the land, but government incentives during the First World War convinced the family to switch to raising sheep. The nearby city of San Angelo was designated the Wool Capital of the world, and the phrase "Cattle for Show, Sheep for Dough" rolled off the tongues of almost every area rancher. The money was good, but running tens of thousands of sheep on a 30,000-acre spread over the course of several decades took its toll, stripping away the native grasses and leaving a hardpan dominated by invasive prickly pear cactus, mesquite trees, and "cedar," as Ashe juniper is known around these parts.

"For the first five years, they could run one hundred animal units to a section," said John Treadwell, a fourth-generation Treadwell. "Now the recommended capacity is thirty-five animal units, but they could get away with [running more than that] for awhile because of the rain." But the historic drought of the 1950s changed local thinking. "The year it never rained, it took awhile [for people] to come around," John recalled. Tens of thousands of Treadwell acres were sold off, leaving the 8,000 acres that would later become known as the Treadwell Roadside Ranch.

The drought and its aftermath left an impression on John. He thought there had to be a better way to manage the land for profit and for the long run. "I remember watching my grandfather and father at the Fort McKavett ranch, thinking, 'These two don't plan ahead,'" John said. "There was no concern for a plan. That was made clear to me when we were told to round up the same pasture we'd rounded up the day before because the registered cows we had sprayed the day before needed to have their chains adjusted because some of them were too tight around their necks. That meant another four hours on horseback."

Planning meant "at breakfast, my dad or granddad would send everybody to where they were supposed to go," he said.

John left the ranch after a hitch in the navy, eventually settling in Dallas. But the ranch was never far from his mind as he was building up enough capital to buy a chain of movie theaters. Returning to the ranch to work cattle remained a possibility, especially after John's father broke his leg, leaving him unable to ride horseback.

In Dallas, John developed a reputation as a gardening expert. He composted like his father did, read up on organic gardening and farming, attended land-use seminars, and made friends with soil conservation agents and state Parks and Wildlife biologists. He embraced the concept of holistic resource management. "Holistic management has these huge charts that allow you to plan six months at a time, or even a year at a time, calculating the size of the pasture, how many grazing days you have," John explained. "It makes you concentrate on making decisions. Otherwise you're flying along until you're out of gas." He read up on Allan Savory, the guru of Holistic Resource Management (HRM), who advocated intensive rotational cattle grazing as a means of healing damaged land and preventing desertification. John joined the state chapter and made friends with HRM ranchers in Texas such as John Hackley and Jim Reed, whose outstanding land stewardship had been recognized by the state.

Trips to the family ranch had etched memories in the mind of John's son, Brian. The time he spent out in the wide-open spaces with his grandparents, uncles, aunts, and cousins set his compass. After graduating from Southern Methodist University with a degree in advertising, Brian produced a hunting show for the Outdoor Channel on cable television called "Runnin' Wild Texas Adventure." He also directed hunting and land conservation videos.

Together, John and Brian talked John's father into doing a prescribed burn at the Treadwell Roadside Ranch. "We all of a sudden had elbow bush growing out of every thicket," Brian said. "That is prime deer food. We had more prairie grass than we noticed before." John and Brian also managed to persuade the family to build a hunting lodge and sell hunting leases for an additional income stream. "Then my grandfather passed away and everybody became a chief," Brian explained.

They found a better path a few years later. In 1996, John Treadwell was made an offer he couldn't refuse to sell his small chain of movie theaters, receiving enough money to make a proposal to Brian: join forces and develop a plan that would eventually lead them both back to the Treadwell Roadside Ranch. Brian, who had been working as a hunting outfitter and outdoor video producer, signed on in a heartbeat.

"We decided if we wanted a family business, we should have a ranch," the strapping, fair-haired, young man said. They looked around until 1999, when they purchased 8,000 hardscrabble acres in Brady in Menard and McCulloch counties on the northwestern fringe of the Texas Hill Country that had been overgrazed and hunted out. Here John and Brian could put theory to practice. What they would learn at their new place, the Treadwell Cattle Company & Rocket T Outfitters, would eventually be applied on the old family homestead.

It was a shaky venture. The ranch had to pay for itself. They didn't have a backup cash reserve, but they had bank payments to make. They were considered a credit risk. "First Ag Credit wouldn't give us a loan because we did not have jobs in town," remembered John.

Armed with a soil map, an aerial map, and a topographic map, they went to work, analyzing soil and deciding where to spend money. Wilkerson Draw was of interest for its expansive watershed and its rich deposits of irrigable soil. They canceled all the hunting leases and built a single hunting lodge. Fifty hunting leases using three unsupervised camps had pounded both the game and the habitat. "Conditions were very poor," Brian said charitably. "It was all brush and bare ground." Behind the wall of brush, though, was some good vegetation—grasses, trees such as Spanish oak and shin oak—overgrazed and mismanaged, but with potential. Eleven water tanks on the ranch had silted in; only one still held water. But three windmills still worked, and thirty acres of the ranch fronted the San Saba River, a much-underutilized source.

The Treadwells opted not to erect a high fence or feed their deer high protein, as was common practice in Texas. Their deer numbers went up, but John recognized that ungulate success was only a small part of the big picture. "It's not only counting deer," he said, embracing HRM talking points. "What is the shape of the grass and forbs that they eat? How does the soil impact the grasses' health?" Too much analysis wasn't enough, as far as he was concerned.

They brought in cattle—mostly a Brangus-Angus mix bred to Black Angus bulls—to browse the forbs and break up the soil. They cleared smart. Chainsaws and bulldozers were put to work sculpting brush and making and cleaning ponds. Downed brush was pushed into windrows that would slow rain runoff and help retain moisture. Solid mesquite forests were eliminated in strips to prevent erosion. They saw wildlife feeding in newly cleared areas.

Most of all, they burned. And burned. And burned. Again and again. They burned so much and so often that locals around Brady and Mason started referring to John and Brian as firebugs. Fire was their favorite tool. Prescribed burns mimicked the prairie fires that were common occurrences before European settlement of the plains. John and Brian had studied burns as a low-cost way of knocking back the dense cedar (Ashe juniper) brakes, prickly pear pastures, and thickets of mesquite trees— giving grasses a better chance of flourishing. When they put theory to work, the results were immediate.

Big prairie grasses that hadn't been seen in decades popped out of the burns. Wilman lovegrass, sideoats, bluestem, green sprangletop, switchgrass, and Indian grass thrived. "They needed fire to germinate," Brian explained. "And when you open up a thicket with fire, there are plants that have been trapped in there that suddenly have access to air, moisture, and light," John added. "We've seen elbow bush, honeysuckle, kidneywood, all kinds of brush species that were invisible." With the cleared areas and the grasses came increased numbers of birds and wildlife. Texas Parks and Wildlife shared costs for the habitat improvement because endangered black-capped vireo nested on the ranch, and rare horned lizards thrived there too.

"There's a saying that goes, 'When you have a hammer, everything looks like a nail.' Our hammer is the burn," Brian said. "It's the solution to so many of the problems you see around here. We started a Calf Creek Burn Co-op that turned into a Menard County Co-op and McCulloch County Co-op. John and I burned more acres before there were these burn regulations and John would tell the Volunteer Fire Department we were going to do a controlled burn and don't come unless we call."

They did eighty burns in seven years on the Treadwell Brady ranch, although "it wasn't until the last couple years we had a good burn that went fence line to fence line," John said.

Prescribed burns and other methods cleared more than 1,000 acres of mesquite and cactus pasture, opening up a 130-acre field for native prairie grasses, a ninety-acre irrigated field, and six food plots ranging in size from four acres to twenty-five acres. The remainder was cleared into brush strips. Another 3,600 acres were cut and cleared of cedar, five new wells were either drilled or re-equipped, twenty-four dirt tanks were sculpted by dozers, and six miles of water lines were laid to fill new water troughs.

"We could've done some of it quicker with herbicides, but John brought us into this borderline organic," Brian said, bragging on his father. "We're natural in everything we do. There's no quick fix anyway," he shrugged. "It is not just a project, but more of a process."

"As much prickly pear as you see now is only 10 percent of what it used to be," John pointed out as they drove through fields inspecting their work. "You want to burn every five years. There will be better quality in the forbs, guaranteed. It started off as burn for grass, but it would take a week to burn through mesquite or prickly pear bottoms. There were high fuel-to-burn ratios. The next year, there was grass there. Where there was hoof action, it came back even quicker. The next year, we'd come back and burn. Every time we did it, we got a result." Using a bulldozer to achieve a similar effect requires ten times as many hours.

Hoof action is the second critical tool they use to mimic historic prairie ecology. "When you think about what the country was like in the 1800s, there were two buffalo herds that came through the area, and there was fire," Brian said. "Our goal was to re-create the buffalo herd through the Savory method of intensive rotational grazing. The place had seven pastures when we bought it. Seven years later, there were twenty-seven. Every time we cut a pasture, we could rest one of our other pastures longer, grow more forage, and expand the number of pastures we could potentially burn."

Cattle provide most of the operation's revenue, although their improved hunting operation is important when the elements don't cooperate. "We had our herd up to 350 when the drought kicked in two years ago," John said. "We had to go down to 100. It took hunting to make our payment." The original herd of 200 white-tailed deer has grown to the point where they need to harvest 200 deer annually to keep the population in check.

The Treadwells were surprised when their efforts began to attract interested outsiders. "The only recognition I've ever gotten was an 'I Make a Difference' T-shirt from my wife," Brian laughed. In 2006, their work on the Treadwell Brady ranch won John and Brian the Sand County Foundation and Texas Parks and Wildlife Department's most prestigious conservation recognition: the Leopold Conservation Award.

Shortly afterward, a "For Sale" sign went up at the gate of the Treadwell Cattle Company & Rocket T Outfitters. John's father had passed away and John's mother would soon be settling her estate among John and his three siblings, including the Treadwell Roadside Ranch. John and Brian wanted to be prepared to buy as much as they could.

But when John's mother hesitated, then decided she wasn't ready to settle the estate or quit running the ranch, John and Brian decided to take advantage of the 1031 tax-free exchange and traded one piece of one investment property—their ranch in Brady—for three others of equal value. They looked near the city of San Angelo, where the Rolling Plains and the Edwards Plateau faded into the Trans-Pecos. Doing their due diligence, they learned from the Texas A&M Real Estate Center that the South Concho River was one of the healthiest rivers in Texas. John purchased a 240-acre farm with 100 acres in irrigation on the South Concho River, fifteen miles south of San Angelo and less than an hour's drive from the family ranch near Fort McKavett. Brian bought a 378-acre farm a mile downstream. They are the two largest water rights holders on the river, allowing them to apply what they had learned about irrigation pivots back at the Treadwell Brady ranch. They also bought 3,207 acres of drier, scrubbier country in Glasscock County near Sterling City, northwest of San Angelo. That ranch had a wind farm contract; as many as eight wind turbines could be constructed, which would generate tens of thousands of dollars in royalties annually. There was enough prime quail habitat to lease portions of the ranch for hunting.

The farms presented very different challenges than the Treadwell Brady ranch did. "Most have more to do with micromanaging resources than reclaiming invaded country," Brian said. But the approach was the same: they studied, consulted (with Howard "The Dirt Doctor" Garrett, Bill Armstrong at the Kerr Wildlife Management Area, and other ranchers), and drew up a year-long plan. Then they went to work again.

John grew oats and alfalfa along with grasses on the two pivots that irrigated his land. Brian grubbed out mesquite and cedar from one hundred acres, plowed it and reseeded it so they could cut hay or graze animals on what once was a cotton field.

"We're trying to learn how to grow the grasses and where the weak links are in our plan," John said.

The Treadwells were also trying to figure out how many cattle their operations could carry and how natural the beef they raise could be. The first year, they used their farms to run stocker cattle for another family. "I had 200 cows on 105 acres from early April until June," John said. "Then I called the owner and told him 'You're going to have to come get these because I'm running out of food.' You can only go around that pivot circle so many times until we learn exactly how many cattle the land can take and still be sustainable. We're working on developing calves from the Glasscock County ranch [near Sterling City] and in fourteen to sixteen months, have grassfat beef that grades high standard and is consistent. And I'm ready to add more stock to my reduced herd, but I don't want to out step myself."

Treadwell Brady Ranch (Photo by Chase Fountain)

They started a large garden, bringing in twenty tons of cotton burr compost to build the soil organically. "It was a third of what we needed," John reported. "But the garden will get bigger and better as we get better at it," he promised. With San Angelo in such close proximity and with plenty of available water, John wants to find out if he can raise produce such as pecans, strawberries, or corn to sell to city folks. "I like the idea of feeding people or working with a restaurant," he said.

"We have year-round grazing and the potential to raise grass-fed beef, lambs, chickens, eggs—if we can learn how to do it. And that is a big 'if.' There are very few places in this country where anybody has mastered raising grassfed animals because from the time that calf is born, it needs to gain a pound and a half each day until it weighs 100 pounds more than its mother. It helps if the mother doesn't weigh 1,500 pounds. If she weighs 1,100 pounds, she's a lot better calving for our operation than those great big cows so many people have. It's a lower-intake, lower-cost cow."

Farming and ranching as naturally as possible to increase profit was part of the plan. "If you can convert to organic, your quality goes way up and, with marketing, can command a higher price," John said. "We got a bonus for our calves because they were natural. They have not received any steroids or implants or hormones or antibiotics. They have been vaccinated. There are people who will buy our calves and pay us a premium for it. But this isn't just a commodity."

Their mantra is, you can never micromanage too much—or know too much. "You keep testing your results against the big picture," John said. For example, they quickly discovered that molasses is a cheaper, more efficient way to deliver nitrogen than chemical fertilizer.

The Sterling City ranch has a lot of good bottom country, big deep soil, and is close to irrigated farms near Garden City. It also has a big canvas of brush.

"We burned this year just out of the need to burn," John grinned. "Remember the hammer?"

They went the extra mile and received official prescribed burn training and certification. They also secured a $1 million insurance policy to do business as a Conservation Fire Team; they do consulting and burning for hire all over West and Central Texas.

Talking, studying, testing, trying to figure out how to best ranch two very different pieces of land are all part of the quest John and Brian have been on for more than a decade now, long enough that whenever doubt is raised over a management strategy regarding a particular piece of dirt, John impulsively utters "Needs a burn" under his breath before the conversation continues. They've had plenty of HRM models to test and are creating new ones to try.

The greater goal, keeping the family-owned Treadwell Roadside Ranch whole and in the family for another one hundred years, remains a distant dream. If and when the call comes, they'll be ready. Knowing what they know will only make it better.

Conclusion

Readers of this book will surely be moved in different ways by the remarkable lives and lessons that leap from its pages. Some readers will be struck by the headlong crash of quiet and humble rural people with twenty-first-century modernity. Some will focus on the almost epic workloads required of family members, young and old alike. Others will be filled with a sense of hope that these and other families across the land can succeed against long odds in their pursuit of sustainability. And, finally, some readers, upon turning the final pages, will be left with reverberations of stoic men and women whose daily engagement with a sometimes capricious and often beautiful natural world has left them with an abiding sense of their own impermanence.

Those who have been tied to a place a while like the Wilsons, the Peters, the Colemans, the Papes, and the Selmans act and speak as wise elders because they earned their wisdom the hard way. Their respect for the natural world and the way they relate to it was developed over the long run. The Langes, the Prices, and the Treadwells accomplished transformative feats in shorter time spans because they had to keep what they'd gained and make use of their knowledge in short order. Everyone has traveled their own path. Several families achieved their goals with the help of additional workers. Most insisted on doing it all themselves. Their politics, religion, and beliefs run the gamut of ideology. And yet they share an independent streak, as well as an uncommon love for the land. For all of them, sustainability isn't a buzzword, but a way of life.

This book opened with a reference to the tools Aldo Leopold believed were essential to improve land health: axe, plow, cow, fire, and gun. All of these families lean heavily on these tools to leave the land better than they found it. The Treadwells explicitly borrow from Leopold's tool set in management of their Texas properties, especially in management and enhancement by fire. Nearly all of the operations deliberately utilize livestock as a range improvement tool. Terry Peters uses modern versions of the axe to improve Wisconsin's forestland with each cutting. Families including the Selmans, Prices, Colemans, and Papes incorporate hunting into their business and educational missions.

To survive and flourish, the toolboxes of these remarkable families have continually varying inventories: a variety of water structures and management; mechanical and chemical brush control; diverse fencing strategies; livestock breeding technologies; and the latest high-tech computing and mapping equipment. And though each of these is important in different ways at different times, the stories in this book spotlight even more important intangible tools that can't be seen in the field or stored in a barn. Tools like ranch tours for a wide variety of visitors, strong local partnerships, planning, teaching, and sharing stretch the impact and importance of their work beyond the borders of their land. The Lange family and Jaclyn Wilson mined the resources of modern business management to strengthen their operations. Many of them, most notably the Papes, keep detailed diaries to help them understand the deeper signals from the land and to be mindful of lessons learned by previous generations. Similarly, Gary Price emphasizes patiently watching and listening to achieve greater ecological awareness.

The stories of these families offer ideas that can be applied by other landowners and even by city dwellers and suburbanites. Most of the *Generations on the Land* families begin with the basic tenet that making a living from the land requires hard work, a stubborn commitment, knowledge accumulated over generations, openness to new ideas, and a willingness to adapt to changing conditions. That each of these families has figured out how to prosper against all natural and manmade odds earned them recognition. That they continue to look for better, even novel, solutions is a rare human quality worthy of continuous praise.

Each and every family member in these unforgettable stories rein-forces who we are as Americans and as people. The land they live and work on defines our nation to the rest of the world. Knowing how they have lived their lives and how they inspired and supported one another should make us want to live our lives better and make our place in the world as good as it can be, each and every day, living more nearly in harmony with the earth that we all share.

Index

Akiyoshi, David, 76
alternative fuels: biofuel, 51; flex-fuel, 44; glycol, 71; recycled (used) oil, 58; sawdust, 44
Altoona, Pennsylvania, 56
Apostle Islands, 51
Armstrong, Bill, 100
Ashland, Wisconsin, 50
Athens, Texas, 26
Audubon Society, 12

Bad River, 51
Bad River Watershed Association, 41, 50
Bean, Michael, 74
Bear River Valley (Utah), 5, 8, 10
Blackland Prairie, 15, 21
Blooming Grove, Texas, 17–18, 19
Blooming Grove Elementary School, 19, 26
Blooming Grove Future Farmers of America, 22
Bluebonnet Resources Corporation, 22
Boren, Ashley, 66
Box Elder County, Utah, 5, 12
Box Elder County Conservation District (Utah), 4
Brady, Texas, 96, 97, 99

Brakel, Kelly, 68, 69
Brazil, 31, 45
Bridgerland Audubon Society, 10
Bridger-Teton National Forest, 83
brush control, 22, 85, 88, 96–98, 102, 106. *See also* plants: *native:* prickly pear (cactus), sagebrush; *trees:* Ashe Juniper, locust, mesquite
Bureau of Land Management (BLM): grazing board, 8; land managed by, 59; leases/permits, 11, 58
burning (as range-improvement tool). *See under* fire (as range-improvement tool)
Burns Forestry, 47

Cache County, Utah, 5, 12
Calf Creek Burn Co-op, 98
California Polytechnical State University (Cal Poly), 76
carbon footprint, 73
Caroline Lake (Wisconsin), 51
Cassiopeia, 77
cattle breeds and breeding: Angus, 20; artificial insemination (AI), 35, 56, 63; Black Angus, 56, 57, 97; Brahma (Brahman), 18, 20; Brangus-Angus, 97; Brangus-

Selman family, 105, 106; from generation to generation, 8, 10. *See also main entries for individual Selman family members*

Selman Ranch or Harold Selman, Inc., 5, 10; and "Birdy Day," 12; and cattle operation, 11–12; conservation easement, 11, 12; federal land leases (grazing permits), 6, 8, 9–10, 11–12, 13; and grazing as management tool, 106; and hoof action (as management tool), 13; and land fragmentation (urbanization), 5; predator control, 7, 9; and sheep vs. cattle, 8, 10; and sheep-raising operation, 6, 11–12; stewardship, 3, 5, 13; water management, 10, 12

Selman, Bret (son of Fred), *2*, 6, 10; and the Audubon Society, 10, 12; the listening/talking exchange of, 6–7, 12; and reading the landscape, 13; and sheep-raising operation, 6; and watering facility, 10

Selman, Cole (son of Bret), 7, 10

Selman, Dean (brother of Fred), 10

Selman, Dorthella (mother of Fred), 8

Selman, Elke (daughter of Bret), 10

Selman, Fred (current patriarch of the Selman family), *2*, 3, 6, 8; and livestock management, 10–11

Selman, Harold (father of Fred), 5, 7

Selman, John (grandfather of Fred), 8

Selman, Jonie (daughter of Fred and Laura), 10

Selman, Julia (daughter of Bret), 10

Selman, Kristy (daughter of Fred and Laura), 10

Selman, Laura (wife of Fred), *2*, 3–4, 5; and "Birdy Day," 12; and the Nature Conservancy, 11; pick-your-own garden of, 6; and stewardship, 13

Selman, Michelle (wife of Bret), *2*, 10

Selman, Wyatt (son of Bret), 7, 10

Serengeti, 82

77 Ranch (Price family ranch), 15, *17, 23;* native (virgin) prairie, 17; habitat monocultures, 24; and decline in bobwhite populations, 23–24. *See also main entries for individual Price family members*

Sierra Nevada aquifer, 69

Sigurd Olson Environmental Institute, 41, 50

Sikkim (India), 77

sheep. *See under* livestock

Sonoma County, California, 74

South Concho River, Texas, 99

Southern Methodist University, 95

St. John (Elementary School), Dallas, 26

Sterling City, Texas, 100, 102

stewardship (of the land), viii, xi; Coleman family, 56, 63; John Hackley, 95; Lange family, 66, 74; Lee Low, 18; Pape family, 89; Peters family, 50; Price family, 15–16, 18, 27; Jim Reed, 95; Selman family, 3, 5–6, 13; Treadwell family, 92; Wilson family, 38–39

sustainable agriculture, 105; in cattle raising, 3, 24, 100; in forestry,

U.S. Fish & Wildlife Agency, 74
U.S. Forest Service, 10, 13, 60, 62.
    See also National Forest (Rough
    Allotment of)
University of Nebraska, 31
University of Adelaide (Australia),
    76
University of California (UC), Davis,
    76
University of Wyoming, 88
Upper Green River. *See under* Green
    River
Utah Cattlemen's Association, 4
Utah Wool Growers, 4

Wasatch Mountains, 5
water management, 24, 25–26, 59,
    106; and conservation, 25, 36, 59,
    65; use of head gates, 60–61, 83;
    irrigation, 8, 11, 36, 37, 60, 67,
    69, 71, 83, 84, 85, 88, 98–100,
    102; and prairie grasses, 18, 21,
    86; watering facilities, 10, 12,
    35, 57, 59, 60, 61, 83, 88, 96, 98;
    watershed management, 26–27,
    96 (*see also* Bad River Watershed
    Association; Watershed Improve-
    ment Commission; wetlands); and
    water quality, 46
water rights, 59–60, 100; monitoring,
    60–61
Watershed Improvement Commis-
    sion, 57
Western Navarro Bobwhite Restora-
    tion Initiative, 23
wetlands, 32, 51, 82, 84; creation of,
    25–26 71, 83, 86, 88; restoration,
    38, 74

White Rock Lake, Texas, 26
wildlife
birds: black-capped vireo, 97; bob-
    white quail, 23–24; Canada goose,
    82; eagle, 62; magpie, 7; owl, 74;
    pheasant, 7; quail, 100; red-tailed
    hawk, 82; sage-grouse, 82, 83,
    86; Sandhill crane, 82, *87;* sharp-
    tailed grouse, *9, 12;* southwest
    willow flycatcher, 57; white-faced
    ibis ("jack snipes"), 7; wood duck,
    74
fish: trout: brook, 82, habitat of, 46,
    84, rainbow, 82
insects: beetles: 83, dung, 24, valley
    elderberry longhorn, 74; borers:
    chestnut, 45, emerald ash, 45;
    praying mantis, 7; wasp, 7
mammals: antelope: 62, 79, 82, 86,
    pronghorn, 79, 81, 82, 89; buf-
    falo, 21, 32, 93, 98; coyotes, 7, 9,
    69; deer: 6, 62, 88, mule, 13, 81,
    86, white-tailed, 92; elk, 6, 61, 62,
    86; moose, 82; rabbits, 62; wolf
    (wolves) 7, red, 93.
reptiles: lizards, 62, horned, 97;
    snakes, 62; toads, 62
Wilkerson Draw (Texas), 96
Wilkinson, Cheryl (great-aunt of
    Jaclyn Wilson), 32–33
Wilson family, 105; from generation
    to generation, 31, 32–33. *See also
    main entries for individual Wilson
    family members*
Wilson, Anthony (original home-
    steader), 32
Wilson, Blaine (father of Jaclyn), *28,*
    31, 33; and his brother Bryan,